P9-CRN-580

Creatures of the Sea

Peter Bowen

Marshall Cavendish   London & New York

Picture Credits
Heather Angel 9B
Anthony Bannister 16 35R 39T
Jen and Des Bartlett/Bruce Coleman Endpapers
S. C. Bisserot/Bruce Coleman 25T
R. Boardman 60BR
D. G. Bone 98T
British Antarctic Survey 82 86B
Fred Bruemmer 8TL 100
Jane Burton/Bruce Coleman 6
Jane Burton/Photo Researchers 24T 25B 33LB 37
    58TC 70 71 72 73T 74 79
Colin C. Butler 39B
John Clegg 26B
J. A. L. Cooke 26T 31
Ben Cropp 9T 47 48 60TL
G. Cubitt 45B
P. David/Frank Lane 35L
K. Deacon 40
Colin Doeg 10
D. Faulkner 75
G. S. Giacomelli 29T 29CT
H. Hansein 56 57 61T 63 66
C. Herbert/British Antarctic Survey 92T
Lilo Hess 64 Inset
P. Hill 11 24B 28 30 53 60BC 73B 88 89
E. S. Hobson 8BL 33T 49
C. Howell Jones 44
K. Kenyon 98B 99
Keystone 5
R. Kinne/Photo Researchers 76C 92B
G. Kinns 90B 94C
J. Kohler/Bavaria 94T

A. Margiocco 81
Marineland of Florida/Frank Lane 65
Steve McGutcheon/Frank Lane 97
P. Morris 59
N. Mrosovsky 29CB 29B
G. Mundey 17 18B 42B 60TR 60BL 76T
Natural Science Photo 67
Noailles/Jacana 58T 77
Okapia 36
P. Parks 27T
B. Pengilley 60TC 61C 68
L. Perkins 27B
Photo Library Inc 50
Roy Pinney 64
Popperfoto 14 51
Dr. G. W. Potts 32
L. Lee Rue 91
L. Sillner 78T
E. Slater 95
R. Lewis Smith 96
H. Stellrecht 12 33LT 33RB
J. Tashjian at Tacona Aquarium 80
J. Tashjian at Marineland of the Pacific 86T
R. Taylor 18T 19 41 45T
M. Thurston 93
Time Life Inc. 8BR
J. Van Wormer/Photo Researchers 85
J. P. Varin/Jacana 90T
R. W. Vaughan 94B
J. Warham 84
A. C. Wheeler 8TR
S. Wightman 22
D. P. Wilson 15 20 33LC 34 38 42T 43 54 76B 78B

Edited by Linda Doeser

Published by Marshall Cavendish Publications Limited,
58 Old Compton Street, London W1V 5PA

c Marshall Cavendish Publications Limited 1975

First printing 1975

ISBN 0 85685 132 9

Printed in Great Britain by Jarrold and Sons Limited

Introduction

Life began in the sea and today it provides us with a living history of animal development. Primitive, one-celled organisms which began the long and continuous chain of evolution millions of years ago are still found there today. Living beside them are specimens from almost every class of animal life, from the simple jellyfish to the highly adapted shark, from the little sea urchin to the huge, complex warm-blooded whale. This book studies each group in turn, tracing the network of inter-relationships and the progress of animal evolution.

Creatures of the Sea is also a fascinating study of animal adaptation. The infinite variety of the sea with its changes in salinity, light, depth, temperature and currents is matched by the amazing diversity of the life found there. Each creature is specialized and modified to take full advantage of its ecology and to cope with the particular problems associated with its way of life. The eggs of the brine shrimp will still hatch after they have been dried, boiled and frozen, and the blenny has been known to climb out of the sea to sun itself on nearby rocks.

Superbly illustrated, this book will amaze and absorb you with the intriguing facts it reveals.

Endpapers *Dolphins*
Previous page *Surgeon fish*
This page *Elephant seals*
Next page *Seahorses*

The following system has been used to indicate which pictures the captions refer to:

◀ left	▶ right
▲ top	▼ bottom
◀▲ top left	▶▲ top right
◀▼ bottom left	▶▼ bottom right
◀◀ far left or previous page	
▶▶ far right or next page	
◀◀◀ previous page left	
▶▶▶ next page right	

Contents

Wildlife of the sea

There is no part of the earth's surface that is as rich or as profitable as the sea. It teems with animal life, from its uppermost layers to its deepest parts. Because the sea is composed of a single element, water, it is often thought of as somehow uniform. It is no more uniform than the land, whose element is air. Land animals extract oxygen from the air, but this is in no way connected with the variety of ecological habitats found there. So it is with the sea. Marine animals extract their oxygen from the water, the medium in which they live. But each species of marine animal is specialized to live in its particular watery habitat.

What variations are found in the environment of the sea? Perhaps the amount of light is the first thing that springs to mind. A lot of light is present in surface waters, but the depth to which it can penetrate is only slightly variable, and at a depth of 20 fathoms there is not enough light to support plant life. So some animals are adapted to living in the light, others adapted for a sort of 'twilight' zone, and others spend most of their lives in darkness. The sea also has a wide range of temperature variations, not only the more obvious examples, like warm tropical waters as opposed to cold polar regions, but temperature variations according to depth – warm on top, cold on the bottom, with distinct layers of different temperatures in between. There are the familiar warm and cold currents – the rivers of the sea which have a tremendous effect on local areas. Then there are the variations in the ocean floor – muddy, sandy, rocky, coral-covered and plant-covered. There are undersea mountain ranges and gorges. There are the biologically rich estuaries, where fresh water meets the sea, bringing with it soil, minerals, plant and animal life, and nowadays, pollution.

This will give some idea of the tremendous variations found in the seas of the world. It is therefore not so surprising that the animal life should be so rich and varied. A typical trawl from the North Sea, for example, would yield cod, haddock, whiting, dogfish,

Butterflyfish and Damselfish
This photograph shows two butterflyfish and two damselfish below them. All of them are relatively small bony fish which inhabit tropical waters in and around coral reefs. They are typical of the brightly-coloured inhabitants of this type of environment, and show the bright colours and bizarre patterns exhibited by so many marine animals.

◄ Ringed Seal

The ringed seal is one of the most common seals, and one of the most populous of the marine mammals. It is an inhabitant of the Arctic seas. Its numbers are estimated to be about six million and it has close relatives in the Caspian Sea and Lake Baikal. They prefer fast ice to loose floes, and herds are constantly on the move, seeking cooler water. They eat some fish, but for the most part live on plankton and small invertebrates. They have many natural enemies – polar bears, walruses, Arctic foxes and killer whales – and the young are especially at risk. Ringed seals are also important to the economy of the Eskimo, both for fur and food. The white coats of the pups are especially prized.

◄ **Butterfish** *Pholis gunnellus*
The butterfish takes its name from the fact that it is a very slimy and slippery fish, and therefore difficult to hold. It is a teleost and a native of the coastal waters between the tidemarks of the North Atlantic. Although it is rather eel-like in shape, they are not related.

◄ **Guitarfish**
The guitarfish is a not untypical member of the cartilaginous or elasmobranch fish. This photograph shows one caught in an anti-shark net. The guitarfish has a shape somewhere between that of a shark and that of a ray, but in habits it is much more like the latter, in that it is a bottom dweller, harmless and of little economic importance.

rays, catfish, whelks, cockles, pollack, skate, mackerel, turbot, plaice, gurnard and so on among the fish, and sponges, starfish of fantastic variety, scallops, sea urchins, sea anemones, crabs, lobsters and many other invertebrate animals. And of course a list like this of familiar creatures of the fisheries, does not include animals like sharks, turtles, seals, whales, penguins and many more marine animals.

Animal life in the sea follows the same general pattern as animal life on land. Marine animals are either herbivorous (plant eaters) or carnivorous (meat eaters); a few, the omnivores, eat both. Logically herbivores must outnumber the omnivores. But, in most places light does not penetrate to the ocean floor in sufficient amounts to support life, so what do herbivores feed on? The answer is to be found in plankton. The plants of the open sea, not of the sea bed, are microscopically small. They are suspended in countless billions upon billions in the upper layers – the top ten fathoms or so – where there is enough light for them. Most of them are composed of only a single cell, and they are able to float in the upper layers; a few have twin organelles which either support them or help them to move. These tiny plants provide a food source for vast numbers of small animals of many different kinds – worms, crustaceans, molluscs, the larvae of many kinds of larger sea animals, including fish – all of them no larger than the smallest terrestrial insects. This incredible mass of living organisms is called collectively, the plankton, derived from a Greek word which means 'that which is made to wander'.

◄ **Humpback Whale**
The humpback whale is one of the larger whales. The whales themselves are the largest living mammals. The humpback gets its name from its posture as it arches its back as it dives.

▲ **Sea Urchin**
The sea urchins, one of the most common echinoderms, are found in all marine waters around the world. There are more than 800 species of sea urchin, many of them large and coloured.

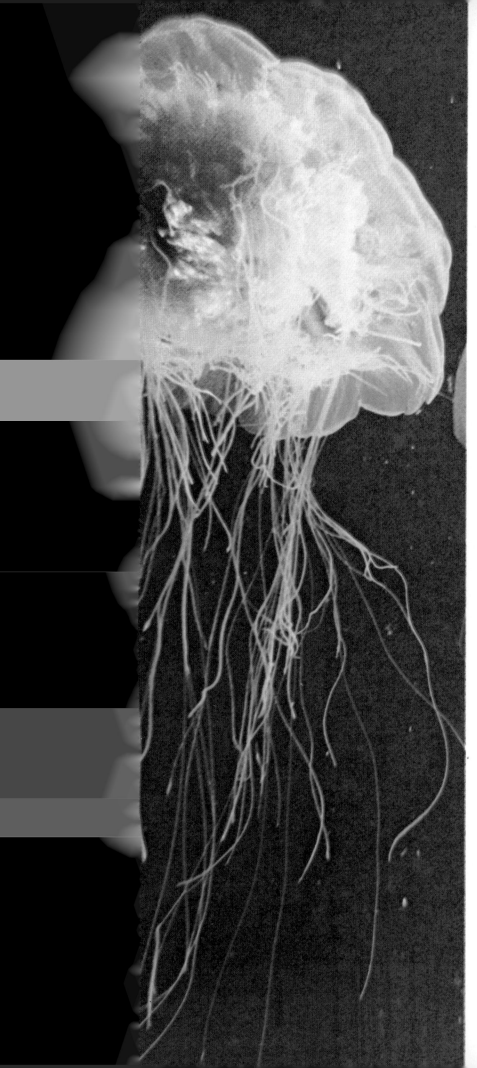

Coelenterates

The coelenterates are a large group of fairly primitive aquatic animals, most of which are found in the sea, although there are a few found in fresh water. Common examples of coelenterates are the jellyfish, the sea anemones and the corals. The coelenterates were an important step in the evolution of animal life. They were the first group to develop tissues – aggregations of cells which perform different functions and co-operate for the general well-being of the animal. This is a significant advance over the primitive single-celled protozoa, in which all physiological functions are carried on by the one cell, and over the first multi-cellular animals, the sponges, which are for the most part aggregations of single cells.

In the coelenterates, the body of the animal is composed of two layers of cells, an outer protective epidermis and an inner lining, the endodermis. Between these two layers of cells is a non-cellular middle layer which is secreted by the epidermis and the endodermis. Certain cells in the bodies of coelenterates have become specialized to perform specific functions. Some cells have become gonads and produce the sex cells. Others are primarily for digestion and secrete enzymes into the central cavity of the body of the animal. Cells of the corals have developed the ability to secrete limestone, building up huge underwater reefs as the colony grows and expands. Certain cells of the epidermis have become specialized for defence and for the capture of prey. These are called nemato-cysts and are cells which contain a tiny dart at the end of a coiled thread. When the cell is stimulated, usually by touch, the dart flies out of the cell and penetrates the object which stimulated it. Poison from the cell body streams down the thread and into the object, which is usually prey or a predator, stinging and anaesthetizing it. There are hundreds of thousands of these nematocysts on a single coelenterate. Most of them are concentrated on the tentacles which are organs specialized for defence and for the capture of food, and are located in a circle around the animal's mouth.

There are three main groups of coelenterates, which are identified by their structure and their habits. The first two of these are the hydrozoa and the scyphozoa.

◄ Jellyfish

The jellyfish is the common name given to the free-swimming members of the coelenterates. In the Scyphozoan coelenterates, the jellyfish, or medusa stage, is the dominant one. Some jellyfish may be very large. This is a photograph of a young so-called sea blubber. This particular animal can grow to the size of a man and the tentacles may be up to 33 times as long again, but it is more usually about half that size when found outside Arctic waters.

When a jellyfish is washed up on the shore, its body does not remain long under the rays of the sun. This is because it is practically all water. In fact, the body contains less than five percent organic matter and about 99 per cent of the animal consists of jelly.

Most coelenterates are small animals, but in many species individual animals are joined together to form larger colonies. The individual members of a colony are called zooids, and they are of two main types. Hydroids or polyps are specialized for feeding, while the medusae are reproductive. In the hydrozoan coelenterates, the mainly sessile polyps, that is, those attached directly by the base, are the dominant stage of the life cycle. They grow and reproduce asexually, but also produce medusae, free-swimming animals which have either male or female gonads for sexual reproduction. In the scyphozoan coelenterates, the medusae are the dominant stage of the life cycle, the polyps being short-lived and inconspicuous.

The third group of coelenterates are the anthozoans. They have no medusae and the polyps become sexually mature. They can be either large individual animals, such as sea anemones, or colonial aggregations of small ones, such as corals. However, none of these descriptions is completely accurate for every species of each group, as certain stages in the life history may be suppressed or absent altogether, as in the Portuguese man-o'-war, a hydrozoan and one of the most complex of the coelenterates.

Coelenterates are for the most part sedentary. Those that are not have only limited swimming powers and drift with the currents. In some coelenterates, muscle cells, such as the tentacles, have been developed, or limited movements of the whole animal are possible. They do not move about in their search for food but trap what comes near them. Any movement they do achieve is brought about by regular pulsations of the bell, the umbrella-shaped part of the animal. This is controlled by a very primitive nervous system and a series of organs around the bell which are sensitive to the pull of gravity, to light and to any chemical substances in the surrounding water.

◄ **Portuguese Man-o'-War**
The Portuguese man-o'-war is one of the most beautiful jellyfish. There are two species of the genus Physalia, one found in the Atlantic, the other in the Pacific. This photograph shows the typical structure. The animal is composed of a colony of four different kinds of polyp. A large bladder-like gas-filled float is the first, usually brightly coloured, under which hang the other three, each type specialized to carry out the particular functions of prey-catching, feeding and reproduction.

►► **Anemone**
The so-called sea anemones were named by investigators who were fooled by their appearance and took them for plants. They have long since been correctly identified as coelenterates, but the plant-like name has persisted. This photograph gives a good idea of the structure of one type of anemone. There is a central stock or body of the animal, which is attached to a suitable solid support by its base. At the other end is the mouth, surrounded by a ring of tentacles which wave gently to and fro in the currents. When suitable prey – a shrimp or small fish, for example – touches one of the tentacles, it is immediately stung and paralyzed by stinging cells in the tentacles. Other tentacles move into action, stinging and holding, slowly conveying the prey towards the mouth, where it is ingested.

◄ **Portuguese Man-o'-War** *Physalia physalis*
This is a photograph of a brightly-coloured specimen
of the Atlantic Portuguese man-o'-war. Its large
inflatable float causes the animal to be blown along the
surface of the water, so although it has no locomotory
ability of its own, it is still quite mobile. The bladder is
filled with a mixture of gases of much the same
composition as air, although lighter, which are secreted
by a gas gland. Muscles in the coat of the bladder
regulate the pressure inside. The bladder is deflated in
storms and the jellyfish rides out the weather beneath the
surface. The float can be re-inflated in a matter of a few
minutes. In rough seas the tentacles are spread out in a
circle around the bladder to help maintain the animal's
balance. The float is always twisting and turning,
dipping below the surface with the action of the waves,
keeping its outer surface moist.

The Portuguese man-o'-war is well known for its
stinging tentacles. The stinging darts or nematocysts,
tiny organelles which are kept in capsules, are located
on the prominent circular rings on these tentacles.
Swimmers who have come in contact with these
tentacles will testify that the darts are capable of
producing an inflammation of the skin similar to that
of a severe burn. It has been estimated that the poison
in a man-o'-war's darts is 75 percent of the strength of
cobra venom, so it is no wonder that they produce so
violent a reaction.

▶ **Sea Fir** *Obelia geniculata*
This colonial hydroid is a common seashore animal, but
is often mistaken for a seaweed. This photograph of one
of the more than 2000 species of this animal, magnifies
a portion of the colony about 60 times, and shows its
structure well. Members of the colony are connected
together by a branching stem, through the centre of
which is a system of intercommunication. The
individual polyps of the colony are the cup-shaped
structures which are supported by stems arising from
the main branch at one end, and provided with a fringe
of tentacles around the mouth at the other end. These
tentacles are mobile and provided with stinging darts, as
in other coelenterates, and are used for catching prey.
Because of the system of intercommunication between
individual members of the colony, it is necessary for only
some polyps to catch prey in order to feed the whole
colony.

Several features are seen in this photograph. The
circular structure with tentacles just below the polyp
at the top-right is the medusa phase of the animal. This
is a free-swimming form, either male or female, which
has been produced by a special sexual generation-
forming apparatus like the one seen immediately to its
left attached to the stalk. The medusa swims away from
the colony and sheds its sex cells, ova or sperm, into the
sea, where they come into contact with their opposite
numbers from other medusae. The fertilized eggs sink to
the bottom and begin to grow into a new colony.

Also seen here are tiny, stalked single-celled
organisms, which have chosen the sea fir as a suitable
base to which to attach themselves.

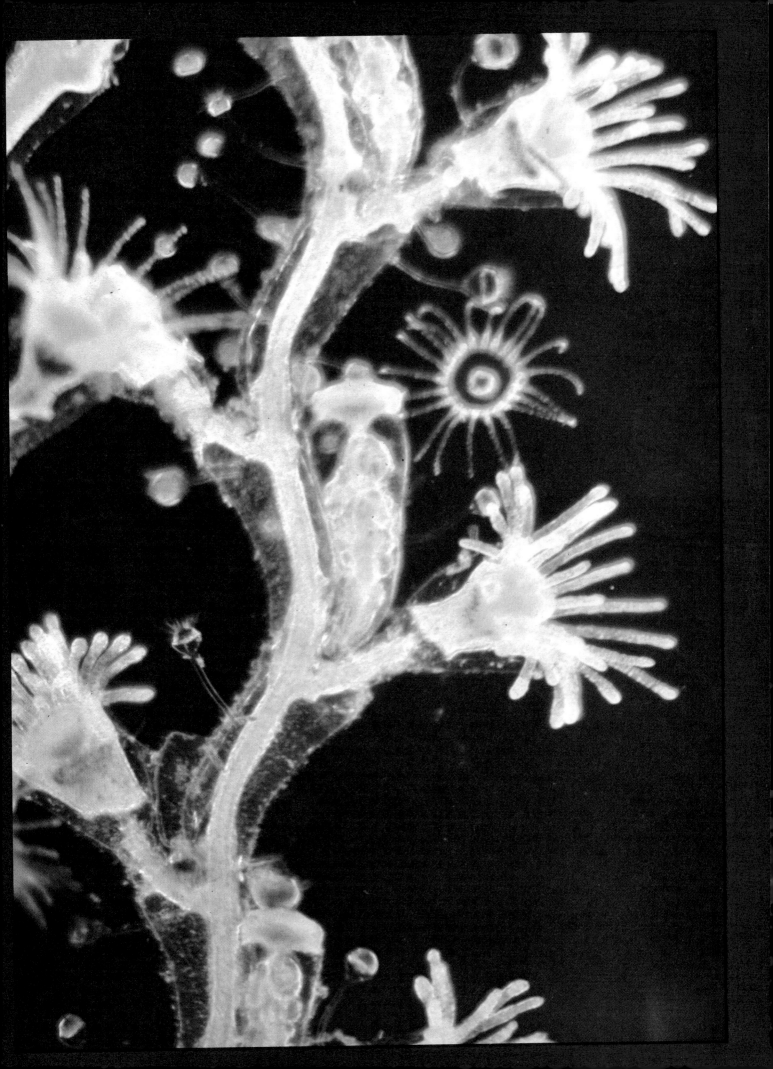

▲ Millepore *Millepora alcicornis*

The millepore is sometimes called the millepore coral because of its superficial resemblance to the true corals and because it is often found on coral reefs. The millepore is made up of colonies of tiny hydroid-like polyps supported by a hard chalky skeleton. Millepores usually form upright columns which branch coarsely. To some extent, the shape of the colony depends on the base on which it lives. It can be plate-like when growing on rocks or similar smooth surfaces, or upright and branching if there is the necessity to grow upwards.

The surface of the millepore is covered with a thin layer of living tissue from which arise thousands of tiny polyps. The polyps can be retracted, if necessary, into tiny holes, and it is the profusion of these openings in the skeleton of the animal that gives it its name of millepore or 'thousand pores'. There are two quite distinct types of polyps, one a short, stout, feeding variety with a mouth and four or more knobs armed with stinging cells, while the other is long and slender, without a mouth but bearing long tentacles with knobs armed with stinging cells for capturing prey. Large stinging cells are also found on the 'body' of the colony. Some species of worms, crustaceans and algae live on millepore colonies.

▶ Anemone

This photograph illustrates one of the many mysteries about the coelenterates. It has been noted that fish coming into contact with the anemone's tentacles cause activation of the stinging cells and the movement of the tentacles inwards towards the mouth to secure the prey and ingest it. It has been determined that both touch and chemical stimuli can cause this activation. Yet here are three clown fish swimming quite freely among the tentacles of an anemone. It appears almost as though the anemone has accustomed itself to the presence of the fish, although the mechanism by which this could happen is hard to imagine. It is possible that the clown fish has developed some sort of protective device that, rather than making it immune to the stings of the anemone, prevents them from discharging in the first place.

Sea anemones are surprisingly mobile. They can grasp the substratum with their tentacles and release their grip at the base, thus being able to move along the ocean floor by a kind of somersault movement. They can also just let go and float away until they settle in a new place. There are even several species of anemones that burrow in the sand or mud. They can survive for a considerable time without food.

Soft Coral

Corals are colonial organizations of polyps, each of which is similar in shape and structure to an anemone, except that it is much smaller. They are supported by an extremely hard, white, calcareous skeleton which, in a dead coral, is white, but which in the living animal takes on the brilliant coloration of the particular species of coral which has deposited it. There are several different types of corals, some of which are called 'tree' corals, but these different groups of coelenterates are separated by relatively minute differences. Basically, there are two types of corals, the reef corals, which form enormous underwater reefs like the 2000 kilometre-long Great Barrier Reef of Australia, and the so-called soft corals, which are illustrated here.

The term soft coral is misleading because only a few corals have any degree of flexibility. The only reason for using the term at all is that it has been used frequently in text books, although even this is not particularly helpful, as it appears that different authors are referring to quite different things when they write about soft corals.

The term soft coral was first used by the Greeks and the Romans. They believed that corals were soft like sponges, when living in the sea, but hardened when they were brought into the air. There are no coral reefs in the Mediterranean, and presumably those which were brought up were in fishermen's nets, so perhaps the confusion is understandable. The first coral to be called a soft coral was Corallium rubrum (illustrated below left), the red or precious coral. Its bright red branching colonies are covered with white polyps with long tentacles, and with smaller polyps without tentacles which lie partly hidden between the tentacular forms. This photograph gives some impression of the wide range of colour, structure and complexity exhibited by these animals.

Most soft corals live in seas from depths of a few millimetres to more than 2000 fathoms although most species are found at 500 fathoms or less. They especially prefer a rocky sea bed for attachment, and are most numerous in the warmer seas, especially the warmest areas of the Indian and Pacific oceans. The size and structure of individual colonies is extremely variable. The colony may be small and low-lying or it may be up to two metres high. In areas in which there is a more or less constant current, the colony will probably be fan-like, its broad side arranged at right angles to the current so that the maximum surface of the colony is exposed to the passage of water containing potential prey. In deeper waters, where there are few currents, the colony may

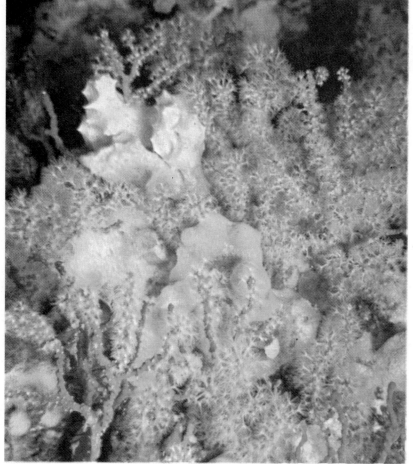

branch in all directions, or form large irregular masses.

The tentacles of each polyp trap any prey that swims into contact with them. The prey is quickly paralyzed by the stinging cells and passed to the mouth. As each polyp is connected to its neighbours, the entire colony can feed on the food caught by a few members, so it is not necessary for each polyp to do its own feeding.

Reproduction, as in many other coelenterates, is both sexual and asexual. Sexual reproduction, in which an egg is fertilized by a sperm, gives rise to a free-swimming larva which moves away from the colony, settles on a suitable substratum and grows into a polyp. Further polyps are produced by asexual reproduction or budding. A bud appears on the side of the polyp which slowly develops into a polyp of the same size as the parent. This process is repeated, and so the colony grows. If for any reason a part of the colony should be broken off, or a single polyp become detached, it will continue to grow and will form a new colony.

Some corals have in the past been regarded as semi-precious. These are particularly the ones in which the hard calcareous skeleton of the colony retains its colour after the death of the polyps, rather than taking its colour from the living polyps. The best known of the semi-precious corals is the red coral of the Mediterranean. It is composed of branching, tree-like colonies. The branches are made of hard red spicules which are firmly cemented together. At one time there was a flourishing industry fishing for the red coral in the Mediterranean, the Red Sea and the Persian Gulf. The red coral lives at depths of from two to one hundred fathoms, so was not difficult to harvest. It was used in commerce and for the making of jewellery.

The so-called tree corals differ from those illustrated here in several ways. They are supported by a hard skeleton which, in life, is covered by a continuous layer of tissue giving the coral its colour. The true or stony corals may be either solitary or colonial. In both cases, the polyps lay down beneath them the hard skeleton which is typical of the corals, in a pattern which is distinctive for each species. The true corals or reef corals are mostly night feeders. During the day the polyps are withdrawn and the surface of the colony is smooth, but at night, as the plankton rise towards the surface to feed, the polyps take in water, swell and stand out on the surface, forming an intricate meshwork of tentacles which trap prey. As in the soft corals, prey is paralyzed by stinging darts, and conveyed to the mouth by the tentacles and also by the cilia which may cover the surface of each polyp.

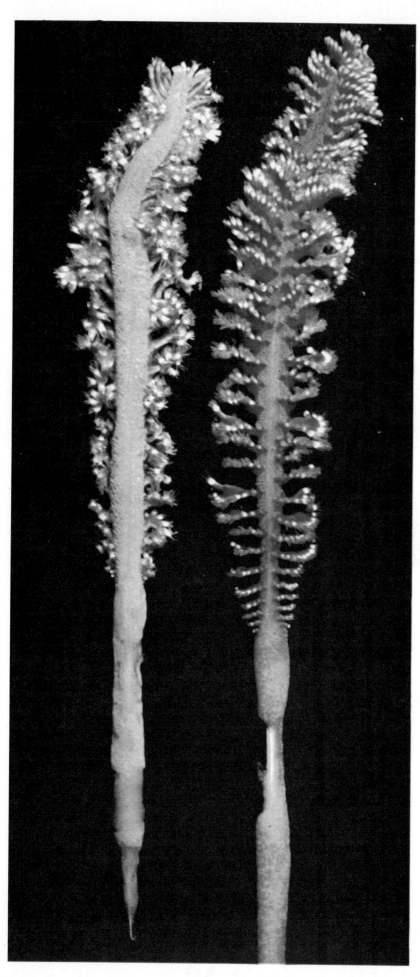

◄ Sea Pen

The sea pens derive their name from the fact that they reminded their discoverers of the old-fashioned quill pens. In fact the sea pens come in a variety of shapes and sizes, some having the common name sea pansies. Basically, though, regardless of shape and size, they all have the same form: a central stem from the top of which protrude polyps or branches bearing polyps. The sea pens begin life as a single polyp which develops from a free-swimming larva. This forms the central stem, and from this bud the secondary polyps. Usually the mouth and tentacles of the primary polyp degenerate, leaving only a stem-like structure which supports the secondary polyps and gets its nourishment from them. A central rod supports the stem and the polyps lay down a complex skeleton of interconnecting spicules which help the colony to remain upright.

The sea pens are close relatives of the anemones and sea firs, and therefore the structure of their polyps is very similar. One peculiar characteristic of the sea pens is their ability to give off light when touched. The light is caused by the release of mucus filled with luminous granules, but the reason for this display, which can be spectacular in a forest of colonies, has not been explained.

► Portuguese Man-o'-War

This photograph gives some indication of the size of prey that this animal can cope with, and is also a particularly good illustration of the crest on the bladder, which acts as a sort of sail when the man-o'-war drifts with the wind and the currents.

Like other coelenterates, the colony begins with a single motile larva. This larva develops into a small bladder with the gas gland at one end. At the other end, the mouth appears, forming the first feeding polyp. Between the two ends the budding zone develops. The first growth from this zone is a stinging tentacle, and this is quickly followed by more feeding polyps and stinging tentacles. Later, the reproductive polyps, some male, the others female, develop. In the meantime, the bladder has continued to grow, and has developed its crest. Growth continues from the budding zone, giving rise to stinging, feeding and reproductive polyps until the animal is ready to breed. Eggs and sperm are shed into the sea, and the colony probably dies at this stage, still only a few months old.

The stinging tentacles may be very long. The darts which they release when prey comes in contact with them penetrate the skin of the prey, fixing it firmly and at the same time providing a tube down which poison can pass to kill the prey. The stinging tentacles are contractile, and once they have captured something, they draw it towards the mouth. As the prey nears the main mass of the animal, the flask-shaped feeding polyps begin to move about. When they touch the prey, they fasten on to it, sucker-like, the many mouths of the feeding polyps completely enclosing large animals and pouring digestive enzymes over it. Small prey can be ingested by a single polyp.

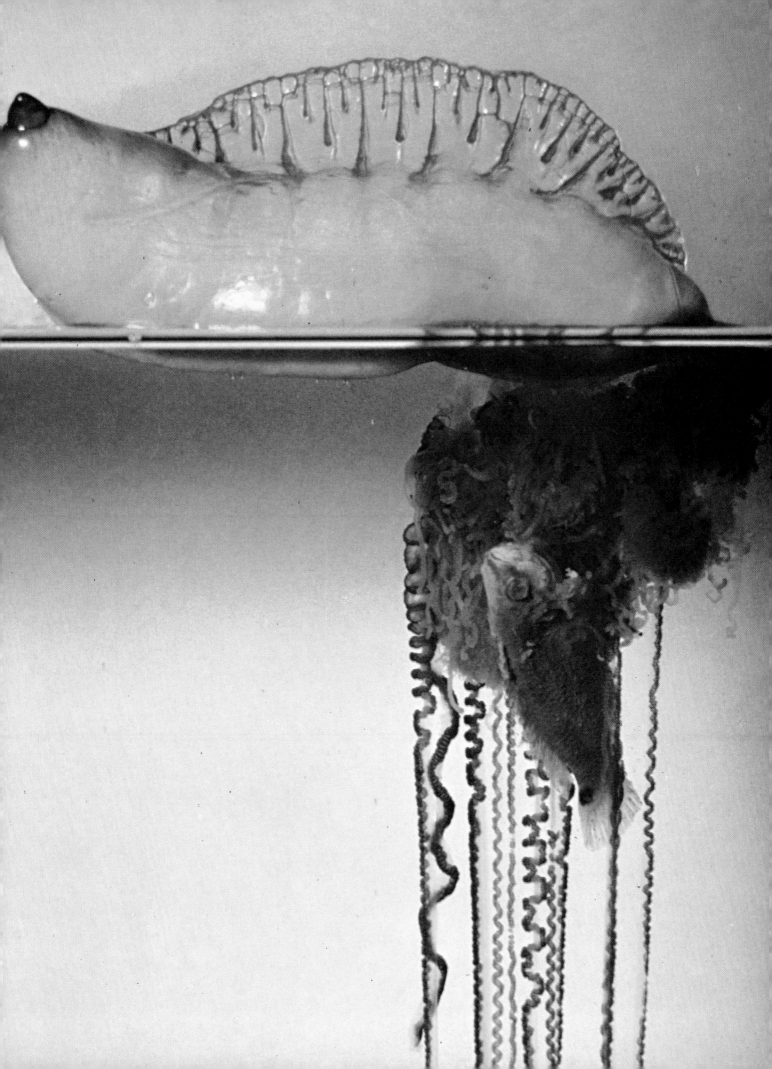

Crustaceans

The crustaceans are some of the aquatic members of the arthropods, the largest group of animals both in numbers of species and of individuals. The arthropods are segmented animals whose bodies are divided into three distinct regions – head, thorax and abdomen. They have a hard external covering, the exoskeleton, which performs many of the same functions as the bony internal skeleton of the vertebrates.

Crustacean arthropods are distinguished from other arthropods by the presence of two pairs of frontal antennae and by the nauplius larva. Crustaceans lay eggs which hatch to produce the nauplius larva, a simple unspecialized sort of crustacean common denominator. Only as it grows and develops is it possible to tell what sort of crustacean it will eventually become.

Crustaceans are much more diverse than is usually assumed. All are aquatic and most are marine, but there are a few fresh-water types such as the cray-fish and the water flea. Marine crustacea include not only the common lobsters, crabs and shrimps, but less obvious members such as fish lice, beach fleas and barnacles, the last often confused with molluscs because of their shell-like exoskeletons. There are even crustacea which have become specialized as internal parasites of other crustacea.

Like other arthropods, crustaceans have to moult from time to time while they are developing and increasing in size. The hard exoskeleton is made of a substance called chitin, which is secreted by glands in the animal's skin. It is not living tissue and cannot stretch to accommodate the increase in size of the animal, so the exoskeleton must be shed. A special secretion called moulting fluid causes the exoskeleton to separate from the epidermis, the outer layer of skin, beneath it. Much of the inner portion of the exoskeleton is digested by special enzymes and is used in the production of the new exoskeleton, which is laid down underneath the old one. At this stage the new exoskeleton is soft and pliable. When all is ready for the moult, the crustacean takes in an enormous amount of water. This causes it to swell and break the now weakened exoskeleton along the middle of the back. The animal climbs out of its old suit of armour, continuing to take up water and swell to enlarge the new exoskeleton and allow for future growth. When it has reached its maximum size, enzymes are secreted by the epidermis to harden the chitin. In many crustacea, limestone from special glands is also added to the chitin at this stage to provide additional hardening. During the moult the crustacean is at its most vulnerable, but once the exoskeleton has hardened it is again well protected from predatory attack.

Squat Lobster

There are four species of squat lobsters, and in spite of their name, they are more closely related to the hermit crabs than to the lobsters. All four species are found in Europe. They live in the tidal zone or in the shallow offshore water, and are very small.

23

◄ Prawn

The prawns are small shrimp-like crustaceans which live in shallow inshore waters. The name was first applied to the common prawn found in European waters, but it has since come to apply to any small, long-bodied crustacean of marine waters. They spend most of their time walking slowly along the sandy inshore bottoms, for like so many of their crustacean relatives, they are scavengers, feeding on any dead animals that they can find, and occasionally taking a bit of seaweed. Some prawns are active hunters, however, hiding in burrows until suitable prey swims past and then either catching it with their large claws or delivering it a blow to stun it, then picking it up. The prawn's most obvious enemy is man, who fishes for it commercially, but most bottom-feeding animals include prawns in their diet. Its principal natural enemy is the cuttlefish. These two photographs on the left are of a common prawn (above) and a so-called piebald prawn (below), one of the more brightly coloured crustaceans common in tropical waters.

► ▲ Shore Crab *Carcinus maenas*

This is the common crab of the western coasts of Europe and the eastern coasts of North America, where it is known as the green crab. Two other shore crabs live along the Pacific coasts of North America, but they are quite different species. The European shore crab is a tough, defensive animal noted for its pugnacious ways. They live in rock pools in the tidal zone and in the sea to a depth of about three fathoms. It is one of the few marine crustaceans commonly found in estuaries and can exist, apparently quite happily, in water which has only 15 percent of the salinity of sea water. It eats a wide range of food, for it is a predator as well as a scavenger, and will eat any kind of animal food that comes its way. The shore crab is particularly notable for having one of the animal kingdom's most complex biological clocks. Laboratory study under constant environmental conditions has shown that shore crabs have peaks of activity which coincide with the times of high tide and the hours of darkness. This means that the shore crab is most active during the periods when it is least vulnerable.

► ▼ Fiddler Crab

The fiddler crab is the common name applied to a group of similar-looking species which are common on tropical sandy or muddy beaches. Only the male has the enormous oversized claw. On the female, both front claws are of normal size. The large claw of the male is so big that it is useless for all practical purposes, and it is therefore assumed to be important for some sort of ritual display. Several theories have been put forward, including use as an attractant for females, especially as it is brightly coloured, and use as a territorial marker. The latter is probably the more likely explanation, as the claw is constantly flashed at other males during low tide, warning them to keep their distance. If a male ventures too close to another, battle ensues, and the large claw is used to flip the opponent over on to his back.

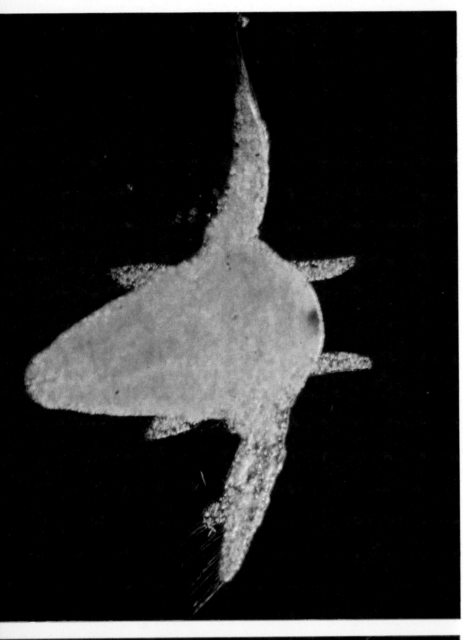

Brine Shrimp *Artemia salina*

◄ The brine shrimp is a small primitive relative of the crabs and lobsters. It lives in salt pools and other very salty waters in many parts of the world, on all continents. It is most common in water whose salt concentration is greater than that of sea water, such as pools, salt lakes and marshes. It feeds on particulate matter suspended in the water, the swimming actions of its 11 pairs of limbs sweeping a current of water towards the mouth where the tiny particles are caught in strainers made of bristles, located along the inner edges of the limbs. Brine shrimps can withstand enormous variations in their environment, from water of less than 0.3 percent salt up to 30 percent. The eggs of the brine shrimp are even more remarkable, for they will withstand complete desiccation, boiling and freezing, hatching a few hours after being placed in salt water at room temperature. This ability of eggs to withstand extreme conditions is doubtless of great survival value, as many of the ponds in which brine shrimps live are liable to dry up, exposing the eggs to the air and the hot sun for long periods until water becomes available again.

Reproduction is also a curious process in brine shrimps. The females have a special brood pouch at the posterior end of the body, and the young larvae, called nauplius larvae (below left), remain in this pouch for up to several weeks if conditions are not favourable to their survival. Under normal conditions, the larvae undergo a series of moults and become mature in about three weeks. In some populations of brine shrimps, males appear to be entirely absent, and reproduction is parthenogenetic, that is, the eggs develop into true adults without being fertilized.

Curiously enough, brine shrimps are not found in the open sea. This is probably because they could not stand the pressure from predators and have instead moved into an environment which most of their would-be predators would find too inhospitable. To cope with the increased salt concentration, the brine shrimp has developed a special physiological mechanism by which salt water is absorbed by the gut but the major portion of the salt content is excreted by special cells located on the gills at the bases of the limbs.

► Daphnia

Although not strictly a creature of the sea, as it is primarily a fresh water animal, Daphnia, the water flea, is worth a brief consideration, as it is one of the smallest crustaceans, the largest of the many species found all over the world being only a few millimetres long. It is a distant relative of the crabs and shrimps, with a hard external skeleton and jointed body and limbs. There is a large central eye at the front of the body, the result of the two eyes joining together during embryological development. The female carries the eggs in a brood pouch under the carapace, and does not lay them unless conditions are favourable. Like the eggs of the brine shrimp, they can survive adverse conditions and hatch years later if the environment is suitable.

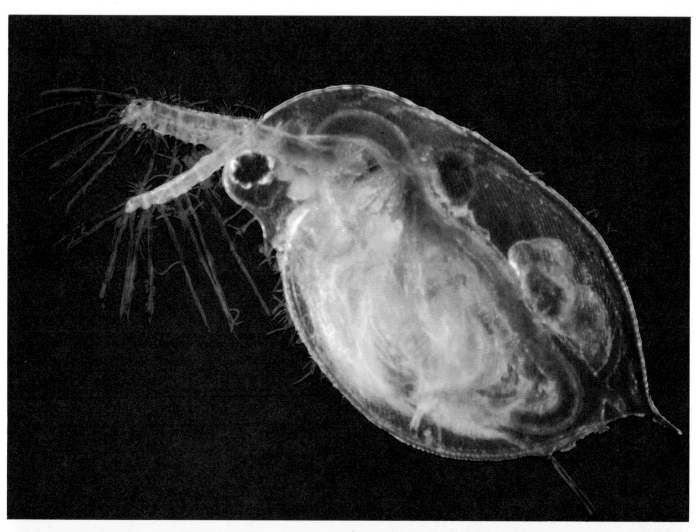

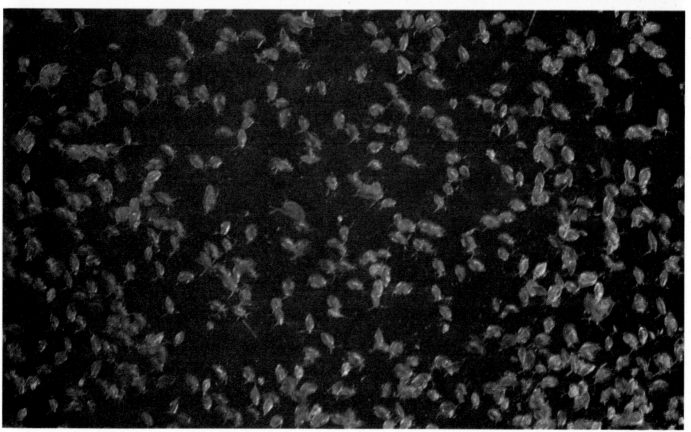

Hermit Crab

There are many different species of hermit crabs found in many parts of the world. Most are marine, but some tropical species are semi-terrestrial. They derive their name from their habit of choosing some alternative protective coat to carry about with them, rather than relying on the tough exoskeleton used by other crustaceans. The most common hermitages chosen by hermit crabs are the empty shells of snails. The shape of the crab's abdomen has become modified and its covering softened to allow it to fit easily into the shell. The front pairs of limbs have similarly become modified for this new way of life. One of the claws is much larger than the other, and is used to seal off the opening of the shell when the crab is threatened. The next two pairs of legs are used for walking. The next two pairs are reduced in size, and are used to grip the shell, while the last pair of abdominal

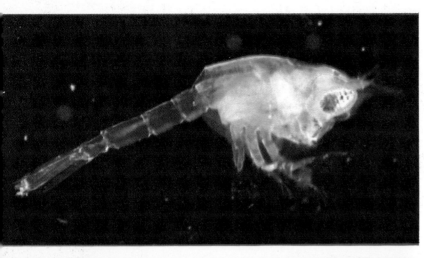

limbs, those which in the lobster form the fan of the tail, are specially shaped to grasp on the central column of the shell. These adaptations make it extremely difficult to remove the crab from its shell. The shell that is usually chosen first is that of a winkle, a topshell or a dog whelk. Normally only young hermit crabs are found on the shore. They are surprisingly nimble, in spite of their heavy load, and can move quickly across the sand. The shell also protects them from being pounded too heavily by the waves, and prevents their drying out. The picture below is a close-up of one of the more common hermit crabs, Pagurus megistos.

The four smaller photographs show different stages and aspects of the life cycle of the hermit crab. Most hermit crabs seem to be in breeding condition for most of the year. The female may carry as many as 10 to 15 thousand fertilized eggs, which are attached to abdominal appendages called swimmerets. The female will come part way out of her shell from time to time to aerate the eggs, fanning her swimmerets to and fro in the water. As soon as an egg hatches the young hermit crab moults and becomes what is known as a zoea larva (top), a tiny shrimp-like animal. This zoea larva lives as a free-swimming animal, undergoing a fairly quick succession of four moults. After the fourth moult, the young hermit crab, which now has the appearance of a miniature adult, seeks its first shell for a home. Once inside the shell, usually that of a species of snail at this stage, the crab is relatively safe from predators. Like all crustaceans, however, the crab must moult periodically as it increases in size. Increase in size means that the crab also outgrows its home and so it is necessary to find a new, larger one. Usually the crab finds a new shell before abandoning the old one, closely inspecting and appearing to measure the new shell as if to make sure it will be large enough. Once the decision is made, the crab leaves the first shell, a split appears along the back of the animal, and it wriggles out of its old skin. As quickly as possible thereafter, it transfers to the new shell, for at this stage the soft-bodied hermit crab is particularly vulnerable to predators. Such a naked crab is shown in the second photograph.

The third photograph on this page shows a hermit crab in the shell of a snail. Part of the shell has been cut away to show how the hermit crab grips the shell with its legs and wraps its soft abdomen around the central coil of the shell. The bottom picture is of the same hermit crab, the shell joined together artificially, apparently none the worse for wear.

Not all hermit crabs make their hermitage in a shell. One East Indian species seems to make use of bits of bamboo, coconut shells and even suitable bits of man-made refuse. One of the West Indian hermit crabs first inhabits a snail shell, but this quickly becomes overgrown by a species of bryozoan, a primitive marine organism, which dissolves the shell and remains to protect the crab and grow with it. Two other species, one West Indian, and the other from the Indian Ocean, make sticks of bamboo serve as their homes. These animals have straight abdomens with a modification to the posterior end which acts as a sort of plug. Still other species do not have mobile homes, but live in holes or crevices in coral or sponge. Some hermit crabs have been known to drive others from their shells in their search for a new home.

▼ Hermit Crab

Strangest of all are the hermit crabs of some tropical regions, which are partly terrestrial. The coconut crab makes a burrow at the base of a coconut tree and lines it with coconut husks. Some of these land-inhabiting hermit crabs may climb bushes in search of plant food, and are reported to rob eggs from nests and to attack young birds. Most hermit crabs are omnivorous, eating just about anything they can find, including a variety of plant food, live animals and carrion.

One of the strangest associations of hermit crabs is with particular species of sea anemones. One or more anemones may be perched on the shell of the crab, and some investigators have suggested that the crab may even go so far as to 'pick' the anemones and place them on its shell. In fact, at least one species of anemone is found only in this kind of association with a hermit crab. This partnership of crab and anemone is one of the better examples of communal living. It is not parasitism because both animals benefit from this association. The anemone picks up bits and pieces of food which the crab tears free from its prey, and is much more mobile because of its association with the crab. The hermit crab carries with it a built-in camouflage, and the stinging darts on the tentacles of the anemone provide an additional defence against would-be predators such as the octopus and squid. One species lives in water which is too deep for light to penetrate, although it has very large eyes. It is thought that the phosphorescent anemone it carries around with it provides enough light for it to find its way.

▶ Prawn

Some prawns are chameleon-like, able to take on the colour of their background. They are able to vary from green on seaweed on the sea floor, to red on red seaweed. By night they are blue, regardless of the colour of their background. This colour change is not a rapid one, as in some other colour-adaptable animals. The change may take up to a week and the prawn first attempts to find a background that is the same colour as its own, rather than adapt itself to its environment. It is only when it cannot do this that it changes colour. The colour change is brought about by hormones. Light entering the prawn's eyes also activates glands in the eyeballs. These are probably different kinds of glands which respond to different colours of light, and the hormones produced by these glands are released into the blood, stimulating the pigment cells in the prawn's skin. Thus red light would stimulate only 'red' glands, and the hormone released by these glands would cause the prawn to produce only red pigment in its skin.

As well as this remarkable ability, some deep sea prawns have light organs. These give out a sort of greenish-yellow light. They are scattered along the sides of the prawn, up to 150 of them on a single animal. The prawn itself may be quite big for some of these deep sea dwellers may reach a length of 30 cm or more. The light organs may flash on and off simultaneously, independently, or in series in a regular progression from head to tail. Man is one of the many predators of the prawn. They are also included in the diets of most bottom-feeding fish.

Molluscs

The molluscs, one of the groups of higher invertebrates, are characterized by having a soft body which is usually, but not always, covered by an external protective shell secreted by the animal. The ventral (stomach-side) of most molluscs is modified to form a large muscular foot for locomotion, and the tongue has a unique rasping device on it called the radula. There are five separate and distinct groups of molluscs. Two of them, the amphineurons, of which the chiton is an example, and the scaphopods, the so-called tooth shells, will not be discussed here. The other three are more familiar, some members having important commercial associations.

The gastropods are the only molluscs found on land as well as in the water. Snails, slugs, whelks, abalones and limpets are members of this group. There are both herbivorous and carnivorous gastropods, with appropriate modifications to the radula according to diet. Most of them move about slowly on their broad and muscular foot, but a few use it as a lever for jumping, while others use it as a fin for swimming.

Torsion, the process by which snails and their relatives develop their characteristic shape, is the most obvious distinguishing feature of the gastropods. They begin embryonic life as a bilaterally symmetrical larva, but at a particular point in development the hind end twists round as much as 180° and comes to lie near the head end. From this point on, development is asymmetrical, and the internal organs on the undeveloping side are frequently suppressed. The body continues to elongate on its dorsal side, forming a spiral pattern which is reflected in the spiral of the shell enclosing the body. Some gastropods have secondarily lost their shells in adapting to new environments and ways of life.

The polycypods are one of the largest groups of molluscs and include all those with paired lateral shells joined together by a dorsal hinge. These so-called bivalves include the clams, oysters, scallops and mussels. The foot is compressed to form a muscular spade for digging and the head is greatly reduced. The two halves of the shell can enclose the body completely in most species, and two strong muscles, the adductors, can hold it tightly closed against predators. The shell is secreted by the inner lining of tissue, the mantle, and therefore is enlarged as the body of the animal gets bigger. The edges of the mantle around the free margins of the shell are kept closely opposed, forming a cavity which contains the gills. At the posterior end, there are two openings in the mantle, the incurrent and excurrent siphons. These may be extended as a long double tube when the animal is buried in mud and are the means by which a constant stream of water is kept moving over the surface of the gills. The lining of the mantle cavity and the surfaces of the gills are covered with minute cilia whose beating keeps the water flowing in a single direction. A mucous sheath secreted by the gills traps food particles such as algae and bacteria which are in the water, and special tracts of other cilia keep this mucus moving towards the mouth where it is swallowed. There is no radula.

The third group, the cephalopods, is very different from other molluscs. At first sight, squid, octopuses, cuttlefish and their relatives do not appear to have anything which would relate them to the others described here. The foot forms a ring of arms and tentacles about the mouth, and they are active, fast-moving animals. Most have no external shell. They have stout horny jaws which assist the radula in tearing food. Their eyes are prominent and image-forming rather than merely light-sensitive. The most primitive members of this group, such as Nautilus, have a secreted external shell, but in other members of the group, the shell has become modified and reduced in size to form an internal supporting structure. The primitive cephalopods dominated the seas for many millions of years, but dwindled to near-extinction. Those that have survived are highly specialized.

▶ **Abalone**
A close relative of the limpet, the abalone is a single-shelled mollusc. The body consists mainly of a muscular foot and is fringed with tentacles. Water is drawn in under the shell, passed over the gills to extract oxygen and exhaled through a line of holes along the top of the shell. Abalones eat seaweeds which they find by probing with sensitive tentacles on their heads. They are scraped up and chewed by the rasping action of the radula. They inhabit Pacific and Mediterranean shores.

▼ **Cockle**
There are almost 200 species of cockle, with a world-wide distribution. The most familiar of these is the so-called edible cockle. It is found from the tidal zone to depths of more than 1300 fathoms, in clean sand, buried below the surface. It is a common animal. In one survey carried out in a favourite habitat, a sheltered bay or estuary, more than 10,000 to the square metre were counted.

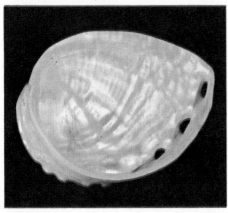

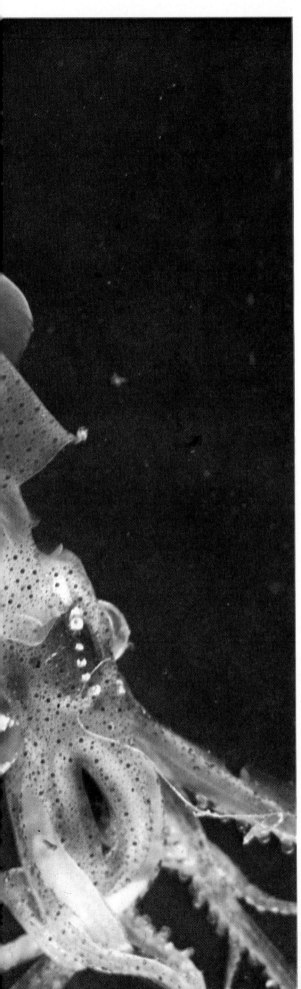

◀◀ Sea Slug *Facelina coronata*

This is another brightly-coloured tropical sea slug. It feeds primarily on sea anemones. The anemone's stinging cells pass through the slug's digestive tract without discharging or causing any damage. They then pass through the tissues of the animal to become lodged in the tentacle-like papillae on the slug's back. The darts collect in special sacs, open to the exterior. The slug has no control over the discharge of the darts as they are not physiologically or anatomically connected to it. But if the sea slug is attacked and one of the papillae is ripped off, the darts will fire. One slug may be damaged by such an attack, but a predator will learn from this experience and in future avoid slugs of the same species. Also its colour may act as warning.

◀ Squid

Squid are cephalopod molluscs. They have two prominent and well-developed eyes which bear a remarkable resemblance to the eyes of mammals. The mantle of the body has two lateral fins and, inside, a supportive structure made of cartilage, the remnant of the mollusc shell. The squid's gills are located beneath the mantle, the layer of tissue which covers the posterior end of the body. It is open at the anterior end and regular muscular pulsations draw water into the cavity, over the gills and expel it again. The water passes through a muscular funnel, and rapid expansion or contraction of this, causes water to move through it with considerable force, allowing the animal to back up or go forward rapidly, an example of animal jet propulsion.

▼ Clam

There is some dispute about which molluscs are clams. Clam is an unspecific word and means different things in different parts of the world. The most obvious parts of the clam are the large hinged shells. They are made of calcium carbonate, deposited by an inner layer of living tissue called the mantle. The mantle is usually extruded along the opening between the shells in a resting, undisturbed animal, and it is a portion of the mantle of the giant clam that is shown in this photograph. The mouth also protects the internal delicate gills. Their surfaces are covered by microscopic extensions of tissue, called cilia, which beat rhythmically, passing a steady stream of water over the gills and aerating them. The gills also collect food.

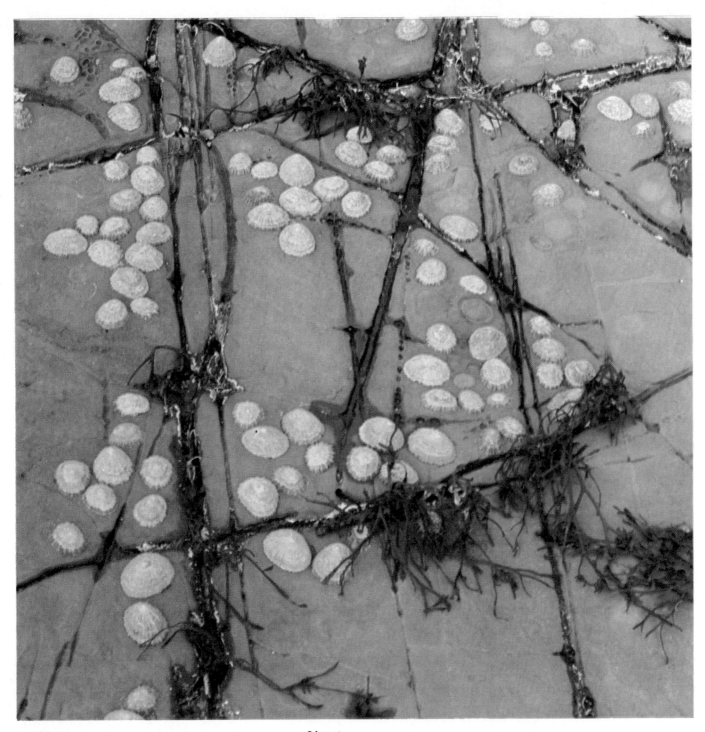

◄ **Octopus**

The name of the octopus partially describes it, for its name means 'eight feet'. The octopus is a relative of the squid and the cuttlefish, but lacks their two long tentacles and the internal remnants of the molluscan shell. The most characteristic feature of the octopus is the long tentacles, joined together by a pliable web at their bases. Each is provided with two more or less parallel rows of suckers which extend the full length of each arm. The body of the animal is short and round, with the mouth at one end, surrounded by the feet. There are more than 135 species of octopus, found in most seas, although they are most common in warm tropical waters. The octopus can disguise itself by changing its colour, extending or curling its tentacles and protruding or concealing its suckers.

▲ **Limpet**

Limpets are relatives of the snails, although at first sight they may not look like it. The name limpet is applied to a variety of different species which have two principal characteristics in common. Their single shell is more or less shaped like half a walnut and they are found clinging tightly to rocks or other surfaces. The limpet shape has evolved separately on several occasions and is particularly well adapted to withstand the hard pounding from heavy surf, to which these animals of the shore line are subject. The body of the limpet is primarily made up of a large, oval foot with a massive flat adhesive surface. There is a distinct head at one end, with prominent tentacles. The shell is lined with a layer of tissue which is called the mantle. The mantle is responsible for depositing the shell.

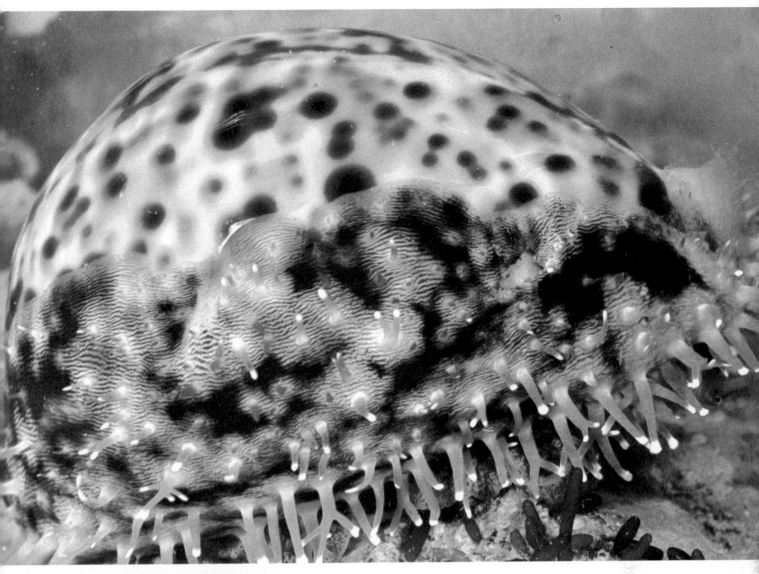

◄ ◄ Sea Slug

This tropical sea slug looks more like a plant than an animal. This is one of several species which eat plant food and put it to more than one use. It feeds on small green seaweeds or algae. These plants have chloroplasts in their cells. These are green and the principal metabolic organelles in plants. When the plant cells are broken down during the slug's digestive processes, the chloroplasts remain intact, passing into pouches which branch off the gut. There they continue their photosynthetic processes, passing their products to the cells of the slug.

Cowrie

The cowries are relatives of the snails and whelks, but they have lost their usual exterior spiral shape common to this group of molluscs. Shown here are two of the more common species of cowrie, the tiger cowrie (above) and the European cowrie (left). When they are moving about in search of food, the outer mantle usually covers the whole shell of the animal. In the picture above, it is forming only a partial cover. There are two sensory tentacles at the anterior end of the animal, each of which may have a light-sensitive eye at its base. In other species, the mantle itself bears a number of small eyes. In addition to eating seaweed, cowries are carnivorous, eating small sea anemones, sponges, sea squirts, corals, other molluscs and a variety of eggs. The breeding habits of some cowries are rather odd. The female lays a capsule containing several hundred fertilized eggs, frequently in close association with a colony of sea squirts. Several capsules may be laid, fertilization taking place at the time of laying by the female releasing sperms which she has stored in a special vesicle after mating. She then guards the eggs until they hatch, within a few weeks. The young cowries are at first free-swimming larvae, but quite soon the shell begins to develop. At first, it grows with the typical spiral but the last whorl overgrows the entire shell.

Echinoderms

Echinoderms are sedentary or slow-moving inhabitants of the ocean floor. They are conspicuous and common everywhere. They are a group of animals which is greatly diverse in form and function, but there are two characteristics which all five groups of echinoderms possess. All are radially symmetrical, that is, symmetrical about a central point, although this symmetry is not as well-developed as it is in the coelenterates. They are pentamerous, their symmetry being in an arrangement of five or multiples of five. The second common characteristic is the possession of tube-feet, hundreds of tiny organs which are used for movement by acting in concert. They are controlled by a remarkable water vascular system.

There are five separate classes of echinoderms, some more familiar than others. The crinoids are the most primitive. They are attached to the ocean floor by a long stalk and the five arms radiate from its top. The sea lily is a good example. The holothuroids are the sea cucumbers, and their common name is the best short description possible. The asteroids are represented by the common and familiar starfish, while their close relatives the brittlestars and basketstars, the ophiuroids, are also five-rayed, but with much longer and more slender arms and smaller central bodies. The last class is the echinoids, again a familiar group, made up of the spiny sea urchins and sand dollars.

The closest living relatives of the echinoderms are a small and relatively insignificant group of animals called the hemichordates. Echinoderm and hemichordate adults bear few common features, but the details of their embryological development are remarkably similar. In the same way, embryological developments in the hemichordates and chordates, the world's dominant group of animals, show almost identical features in some respects. Thus the echinoderms occupy a unique position, for in or near them are the ancestors of the chordates. The possible origins and relationships between the two is one of the most exciting fields of speculation in the whole of zoology.

▶ Featherstar

At first sight the featherstars do not appear to be typical echinoderms because it is difficult to see their basic five-rayed structure. Each of the five arms of the featherstar splits at its base, producing ten arms, each of which in turn subdivides. This gives the impression of a bundle of arms randomly arranged, as in this brilliant yellow featherstar from the Great Barrier Reef. Featherstars are found in most seas, at a depth of about 100 fathoms, on hard bottoms.

▼ Sea Cucumber

There are more than 1000 species of sea cucumbers, the group of echinoderms which look most like plants. The basic five-rayed structure, although present, is not easily seen externally except at the anterior end of the animal. Here the tentacles, not visible in this photograph, are arranged in a circle in multiples of five. Sea cucumbers are found in all seas, in a variety of shapes and sizes to adapt them to a variety of environments.

Brittlestar

The brittlestars are echinoderms which are related, although not particularly closely, to the starfish. There are five long arms radiating from a central body. The body is so small in relation to the length of the arms that it is often called a disc. A large brittlestar may have a disc 10 cm in diameter, although the arms have a span of up to 60 cm. The animal is protected by a hard covering of plates and spines on the disc and the arms. The plates on the arm are articulated, and the muscles of the arm are attached to them, giving supple movement which is not dissimilar to that of the flexing of a mammalian tail. There are many different species of brittlestars. There is one species which seems to be found in almost all marine waters. Other species are less widespread but there are brittlestars of one form or another in all the oceans.

Brittlestars take their name from the fact that their arms fall off, or can be pulled off, very easily. This is not a particularly serious problem, for new appendages grow immediately to replace lost ones. Some brittlestars live on the seabed, and prefer a muddy bottom into which they can burrow. Others live amongst the seaweeds or corals. They are not particularly mobile although they can use two or four arms, working in pairs in a sort of rowing action to propel them across the bottom, or allowing them to 'swing' through the seaweed in an acrobatic fashion.

Brittlestars feed either actively or passively. Passive or filter feeding involves the entrapment of small particles of organic matter or of microscopic organisms, in threads of mucus which extend from the arms. Organic debris and micro-organisms become entangled in the mucus, which is continually pulled back towards the animal by the action of thousands of minute cilia which cover the areas. The ciliary action carries the mucus towards the so-called 'tube feet', a characteristic structure in echinoderms. Their action masses the mucus and passes it from one tube foot to the next. This results in the formation of a mucoid ball which is passed down the arm,

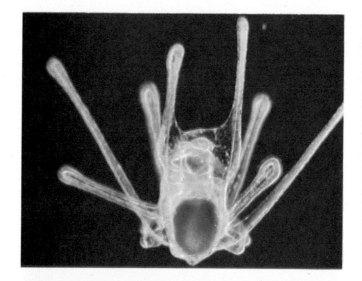

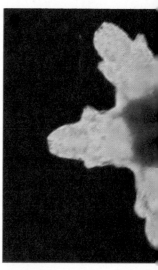

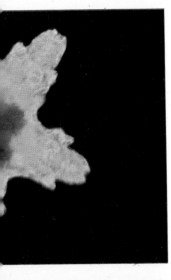

being added to all the time, until it reaches the mouth. Tube feet around the mouth examine the ball, and if it is acceptable, it is ingested. If it is unacceptable it is passed back down the arm and released from the end. The part that the tube feet play in feeding in brittlestars is quite unique, as the tube feet in most echinoderms are concerned with locomotion, and this function, plus their shape, gives them their name.

Breeding is a relatively simple process. In most cases, eggs and sperm are shed into the sea via genital openings at the bases of the arms. Fertilization is therefore external, the fertilized egg developing into a delicate long-armed larva covered with cilia whose action keeps the animal from sinking for quite some time. Two stages of development of the larva are shown at the top. The newly-hatched larva (left) does not bear much resemblance to the adult. By the time the larva has metamorphosed (right), it shows the basic structure of the adult even at this stage, when the tiny brittlestar in this picture has been enlarged to 90 times its actual size. A few species of brittlestar have different breeding habits, in that fertilization is internal, and the larvae are retained inside the body of the female until they have metamorphosed, then being released as miniature adults. Some of these species are hermaphrodites, but self-fertilization is prevented by the fact that the ovaries and testes mature at different times.

◀ **Sea Cucumber**

This brilliantly-coloured sea cucumber, a tropical species from the Great Barrier Reef, gives a better idea of the general structure of this group. It is more or less U-shaped, with the posterior end of the body slightly upturned. The feathered tentacles are particularly well seen at the anterior end of this specimen. Several species of molluscs use the interior of living sea cucumbers as a home, and some, like one species of snail, have become so adapted to this kind of life that they have become reduced to a bag of reproductive organs and nothing else.

▶ **Featherstar**

This photograph gives some idea of the typical posture of most featherstars. The arms radiate out from the central body in a bowl-like formation. Food – organic debris or plankton – drifts into the current to be caught up in the mucoid secretion of the arms.

▼ **Starfish** *Protoreaster lincki*

The starfish are probably the most commonly known of all the echinoderms. The most familiar types are the typically arrayed five-armed specimens, but the number of arms may vary from four to fifty. Size is also variable, ranging from less than 1 cm in the smallest species to more than 90 cm in the largest. This photograph shows a number of specimens of a common species of the Indian Ocean, together with a hermit crab and another common echinoderm, a sea urchin.

Cartilaginous fish

Eagle Ray
This eagle ray, one of several species, derives its name from the fact that its shape is slightly different from that of other rays. Unlike other rays and their relatives the skates, the wing-like pectoral fins do not extend as far forward as the head. The snout and head are left clear, giving the general impression of the shape of an eagle in flight, rather well shown in this picture. There is a long tail, armed with a poison spine, and like the other rays and skates, the mouth and the gill openings are on the underside of the body. Eagle rays are primarily tropical, but they are caught occasionally in temperate waters. Unlike their relatives, the eagle rays do not spend most of the time on or near the bottom of the sea, but seem to prefer to spend their time swimming gracefully through the upper layers of the sea, occasionally breaking the surface of the ocean and skimming short distances over the surface before descending again.

It is important, at the outset, to define just what is meant by the word fish. Some people seem to apply it to any aquatic vertebrates, and some even apply it to aquatic mammals, in expressions like 'whale fish'. Others refer to various aquatic invertebrates – crustaceans, molluscs and echinoderms – as fish. 'Fish' is not a scientific term, but strictly speaking it should be used to describe aquatic chordates which have fins and gills.

Using this definition, there are three living groups of fish and a good fossil record to determine their relationships with their extinct ancestors and relatives. First, what is the difference between a chordate and a vertebrate? Chordates are animals which have, at some stage in their lives, a long dorsal rod of tissue called the notochord, which serves to stiffen and support the body, gill pouches in the pharynx and a single, dorsal tubular nerve cord. Vertebrates have a cranium encasing the brain and separate vertebrae in the backbone, replacing in the adult the more primitive notochord. Thus all vertebrates are chordates, but not all chordates are vertebrates.

The origins of the chordates, which gave rise to the vertebrates, are not clear, but as pointed out in the section on echinoderms, they probably came from a relatively obscure and now extinct echinoderm-like ancestor. The record of the subsequent evolution of the vertebrates is now reasonably complete. The most primitive were small, fresh-water, bottom-feeding animals called the agnathans, meaning jawless. They were generally fish-like in appearance, had a thick armour of bony plates and scales below the surface of the skin and a skeleton made of cartilage. They had median but no paired fins, a single median nostril, a pair of lateral eyes and a third light-sensitive, but probably not image-forming eye called the pineal eye. They had several to many pairs of gills, and in most species there was a separate gill slit, or opening to the exterior, for each gill. The only living members of the agnathans are the lampreys and the hagfish, known as cyclostomes because of their circular, jawless mouths. They are primitive vertebrates in many respects, but they are modified and degenerate offshoots.

The next most primitive group of living vertebrates are the skates and rays, the cartilaginous or elasmobranch fishes. They represent a significant advance over the agnathans. They have jaws and paired fins, well-developed scales, are hydrodynamically designed to fit their habitat and behaviour, and a reduced number of gills and gill slits. Like their more primitive ancestors, they evolved in fresh water and then invaded the sea, so that most living elasmobranchs are marine. The skeleton of the sharks, dogfishes, skates and rays is primitive in many respects, but the fact that it is made of cartilage and not of bone is not a primitive characteristic. The elasmobranchs have evolved from ancestors with bony skeletons, and the presence of the cartilaginous skeleton is a retrograde condition.

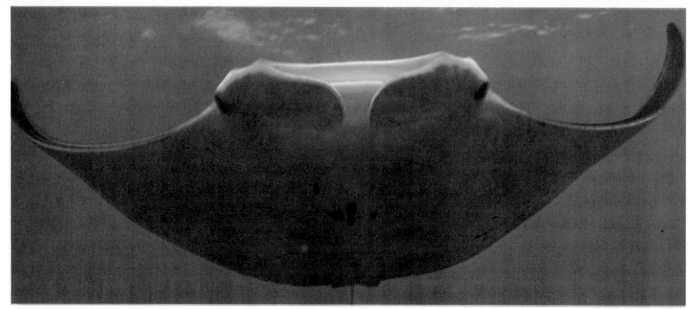

Devil Fish

There are fewer than 20 species of devil fish, probably
better known by their more common, if slightly
inaccurate name of manta. The mantas are some of the
largest rays and may have a 'wing span' of more than
20 m and can weigh as much as a rhinoceros. The typical
ray shape of a flattened body, wing-like pectoral fins
and a long tail, in some equipped with a poisonous spine,
is slightly altered in the devil fish by having an anterior,
rather than underside mouth, which is relatively large
(left). The 'horns' at either side of the mouth are formed
from extensions of the pectoral fins. Like the eagle rays,
mantas spend a good deal of their time in the upper
waters of tropical and sub-tropical seas. Their bat-like
flight has prompted a series of common names referring
to this characteristic movement – sea bat, batfish and
vampire ray. Unlike some species, these rays may form
schools (above), although they are more usually
solitary or in pairs.

Devil fish are filter feeders, in spite of their large size
and predator-like appearance. They swim through water
rich in planktonic food, and a special filtering system
removes the food from the water before it passes over the
gills to the exterior, and channels the food into the
oesophagus. Because of their size and appearance, devil
fish have a bad reputation, but this is probably for the
most part untrue. A leaping devil fish can smash a small
boat if it lands on it, or tow a boat if it has been
harpooned, but these are the results of either deliberate
interference with the animal or an inadvertent move on
its part. Because of their size, they have been difficult
to study, but evidence from skindivers indicates that
devil fish are for the most part gentle, inquisitive
creatures, with no malicious streak in them. This is
probably illustrated by the fact that divers can hold on to a
swimming devil fish and hitch a ride with it for some
considerable distance.

During mating, the male and female swim together
and seem to embrace each other with their large
pectoral fins. Usually, only one young is born at a
time but it is quite large and very well-developed
at birth.

◀ **Sand Shark**

The sharks are probably the most feared of all the marine animals, but only partly for good reason. They are for the most part active predators and they are certainly known to attack man. This photograph illustrates particularly well the structure of the shark's mouth. It is provided with sharp teeth, and the position of the large mouth makes it necessary for the animal to roll over on its side or back to make an attack. Attached to the underside of this shark is a remora, a bony fish whose first dorsal fin has become adapted into a powerful sucker.

▼ **Skate**

There are more than 100 species of skate, one of the more familiar cartilaginous fish because of its commercial importance. Skates are amongst the smallest group of the rays but externally the close relationship is obvious. Skates are for the most part bottom dwellers, feeding on crustaceans and small fish, which they capture with a pouncing movement, so smothering them with their large pectoral fins and then attacking with the mouth. Like some other marine animals, skates have organs in their tails, producing an electrical charge of about four volts.

Bony fish

As mentioned in the previous section, the sharks and similar fish were fresh water animals in the first instance, as were the first vertebrates. They subsequently developed the physiological mechanisms which allowed them to enter and exploit salt water environments, then under the domination of the giant cephalopod molluscs. While this was going on, and the elasmobranchs or cartilaginous fish, were establishing themselves as the dominant form of marine animal life, another offshoot of the primitive vertebrates, the bony fish, was developing rapidly and becoming dominant in fresh water.

The bony fish resemble their cartilaginous relatives in being evolutionarily advanced fishes. They have efficient paired appendages, the pectoral and pelvic fins, for balance and fine movement, powerful tail and body muscles for propulsion, and strong jaws with teeth. Most obvious, perhaps, is the presence of a bony skeleton which has replaced the more primitive cartilage. In embryological development, the skeleton is first laid down as cartilage and is then eroded and replaced by bone.

Two other characteristics indicate the evolutionary superiority of the bony fish. The first is the presence of the operculum, a bony flap which covers the gills and reduces the number of external openings of the gill chambers to one on each side. The second is the presence of the swim bladder, a usually single, blind, median, gas-filled sac which is an outpouching of the pharynx. For many years it was believed that the swim bladder was the evolutionary precursor of the lungs of the higher vertebrates, but the reverse is probably more likely. Lungs probably developed in early freshwater fish to enable them to survive in stagnant water or during drought, as in the living lungfish of Africa, South America and Australia. Thus the freshwater bony fishes which invaded the sea probably had at least rudimentary lungs, which had enabled them to survive the unreliable freshwater conditions which had occurred earlier. Those freshwater fish that did not have lungs either became extinct or, like the sharks, moved to the sea. Life in the sea presents its problems, but not droughts. Therefore the lungs are relatively useless for respiration, but have become adapted, as swim bladders, to function as hydrostatic organs. By secreting gas into, or absorbing gas from, the swim bladder, the fish can adjust its specific gravity, and thus is able to maintain itself at varying depths in the water with minimal effort.

Scorpionfish

The 300 or so species of scorpionfish include some of the most beautiful as well as some of the ugliest bony fish. Their special appearance is due to two particular features. The head is massive, with the eyes high and the mouth wide and downward-sloping. The fins are divided into narrow strips supported by spines. There are also numerous poison spines scattered amongst the fins. The body is usually covered with brightly coloured stripes. Most scorpionfish are found in temperate seas, although there are a few natives of the tropics.

▶ Scad *Trachurus trachurus*

*The scads were originally known as horse mackerel,
but although the two do look alike, there are several
differences which warrant the separation of the two
species. There are three species of scad and the one shown
here is the common scad, a native of the North Atlantic.
It is most common in European waters but is also found
off the coast of North America. The other two species
of the genus Trachurus are also found in the North
Atlantic as well as in the Mediterranean and Black Seas.*

*The scad are identified by their torpedo-like shape.
They have a prominent lateral line, well shown in this
photograph. The lateral line is a sensory organ found in
all the fish-like aquatic vertebrates and runs from the
head to the tail. It is provided with minute sensory cells
which are sensitive to low frequency vibrations,
movement and perhaps to pressure changes in the water,
telling the fish what depth it is at. In the scad, the lateral
line is covered by a series of small bony plates and is one
of the fish's distinguishing characteristics.*

*Scad spawn in the North Atlantic during the summer
months. The eggs have a relatively high acid content, so
that they float near the surface of the water until
hatching. The young larva is small and finless. Young
scad feed on diatoms and other plankton such as larvae
of fish and crustaceans, and eggs of a variety of types of
animals. As they grow older, they form into schools or
shoals. They continue to be carnivorous, feeding on
other fishes such an anchovies, herrings, sprats and
pilchards. They will also eat molluscs such as squid, and
crustaceans.*

*Scad have little or no economic importance as a food
fish. Large commercial fisheries do exist off the coats of
Portugal and Spain, where they are eaten, but for the
most part they are used to make fish meal.*

*There is no definite information as to the predators
of the scad, but it seems most likely that these would
include larger, carnivorous, bony fish as well as
porpoises and dolphins. Scad have developed the habit
of seeking shelter among the tentacles of certain
jellyfish. Presumably they themselves are immune to the
sting of the nematocysts, and it has been reported,
although not confirmed, that they eat the tentacles and
even the eggs. They also prey on other aquatic animals
which seek refuge among the jellyfish's tentacles.*

▶▶ Stonefish

The stonefish is almost certainly the ugliest of all the bony fish, and is doubtless the most poisonous. The head is broad and flat, rather like that of the toadfish, and the body tapers rapidly to the tail. The mouth is large and wide. The skin is scaleless and is covered with warts and bumps which are in turn covered by a layer of mucus. The stonefish is able to vary its coloration in relation to its background, so that it can be mud-coloured, stone-coloured, or even like a variety of types of seaweed. There are three species of stonefish, extending from the Red Sea to East Africa, India and the coasts of Australia, and they are found in shallow seas on rocky, coral-covered, or muddy bottoms.

The stonefish's principal defence, other than its superb camouflage, is its powerful, even lethal, poison. The fin rays, bony extensions which support the fins, have become adapted as poison spines. There are 13 of these spines along the dorsal fin, three on the anal fin, and one on each of the pelvic fins, giving the stonefish all-round protection. Each spine has two poison sacs near its tip. The spine is covered with a sheath of skin, but pressure on the tip of the spine causes the sheath to slide back, exposing the needle-sharp shaft. This has two grooves in it leading to the poison sacs. The poison flows along these grooves and into the wound. When disturbed, the stonefish lies completely still, the only movement being the almost undetectable erection of the spines. Even when caught the stonefish is still dangerous, for it can stay alive for up to 10 hours out of water, and even when dead can still inflict a serious injury, as the method of delivering the poison is purely passive. Although some reports of swimmers tangling with stonefish have noted little or no damage, there are well-authenticated cases of agonizing pain, and even death, from a large dose of stonefish poison. Part of the variation from person to person in reacting to the poison is probably explained by the likelihood that some people are more sensitive to the poison than others, in the same way that different people have varying degrees of reaction to mosquito bites. The stonefish is carnivorous, lying quietly on the bottom until suitable prey swims past, then grabbing it with its large mouth. The stonefish's move is so fast the prey just seems to disappear. Surprisingly, perhaps, the stonefish does have a few predators including sharks.

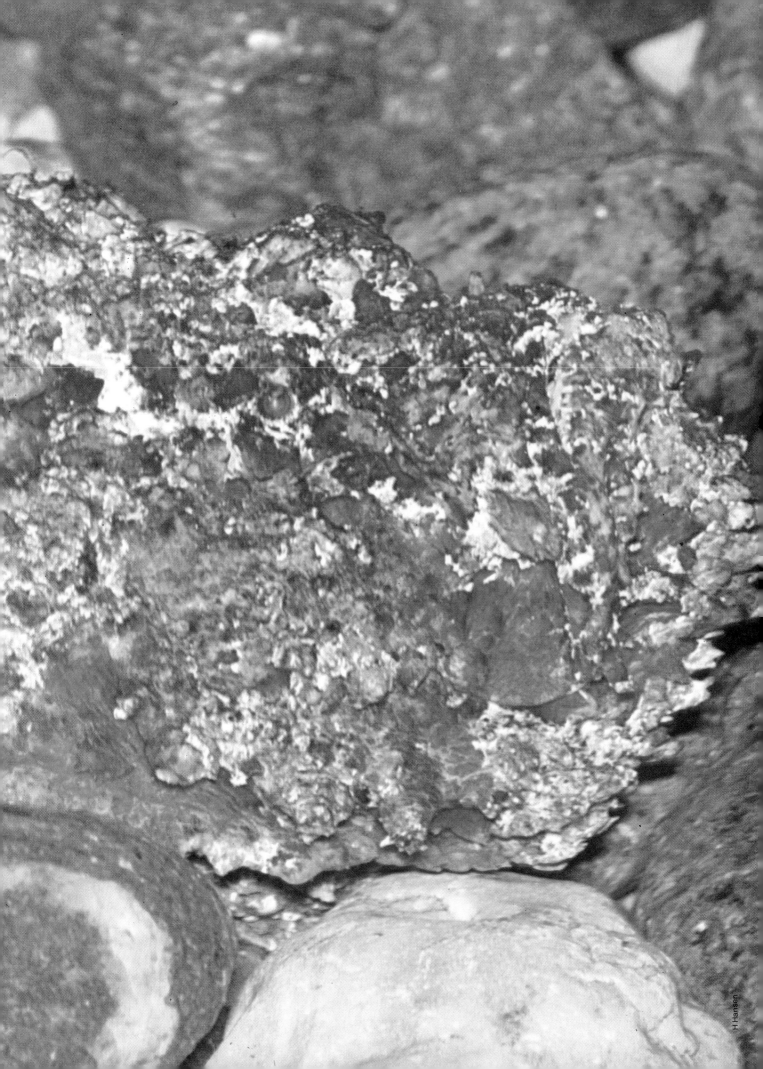

H Hansen

▶ Mullet

This is a school of young mullet, or fry, stranded in a pool. Pools are frequently inhabited by young mullet, who presumably are protected from predators in this way for at least part of every day. Mullet spawn in shallow water, clustering together tightly. The eggs hatch quickly and the young fry begin to feed. They live together in shoals during the day, dispersing at night with each fish going to its own spot on the ocean floor. Any disturbance will cause them to form quickly into the shoal once more. They are primarily filter feeders, sucking up sand and mud into their mouths and extracting the organic material from it by a sophisticated filtering system. They spit out the inedible portion. They also feed at the surface, again using a filtering system, and are particularly numerous when the tide is running out, picking up small animals and particles of food as they are swept out to sea. As well as having taste buds inside their mouths, they have them scattered over the outer surface, especially the head. They also eat small crustaceans and carrion and will scrape small filaments of algae off stones, piers and other solid objects under water. Mullet are tropical and sub-tropical fish moving into temperate waters in the summer months.

Gurnard

There is one particular feature which separates the gurnards, or sea robins (left and below), from all other fish. This is the two or three rays of the wing-like pectoral fins which are separated out to form tentacle-like feelers. These serve two purposes, the first of which is locomotion. The gurnards are bottom dwellers for the most part, and their movement across the ocean floor is almost entirely due to these feelers which they use in the same manner as a punt pole. They lift the body of the fish off the floor, moving it forwards, backwards or sideways as it progresses across the rocky or muddy bottom. The pectoral fins themselves, as well as the anteriorly-placed pelvic fins, are held close to the body during this kind of movement and are used mainly for balancing.

The other use of these false legs is sensory. Most fish have in their mouths, on their lips, tongues and heads, cells which are sensitive to chemical stimuli, used for discovering food sources. However, in these bottom-dwelling gurnards, these sensory cells are concentrated on the feelers, which they use to detect their prey, mostly small crustaceans, small fish and sand eels.

Gurnards are also notable for their habit of grunting. When they are removed from the water, distinct grunting noises can be heard, some of them most vocal during the breeding season. The noise is made by the contraction of the swim-bladder, by special muscles.

▲ Moray Eels

There are about 120 species of moray eels, of which six are shown above. They are inhabitants of warm seas in tropical and sub-tropical areas, living on or near coral reefs at depths of up to 15 fathoms. Although the eels are true bony fish, or teleosts, they have several interesting anatomical modifications which separate them from most other teleosts. The skin is thick and the scales have been lost. In some species, the dorsal fin has become greatly enlarged, and may start just behind the head, as can be seen in some of these photographs. In other species the dorsal, tail and anal fins may be absent. In all eels, the pectoral and pelvic fins are either greatly reduced or absent, as in the morays. These modifications to some fins and loss of others, combined with the greatly elongated jaws, give the eels in general, and the morays in particular, a marked, snake-like appearance.

It is probably their appearance, rather than their actual behaviour, which has given the morays a fierce and sinister reputation. Like most snakes, they do not appear to deserve it. Stories are told of them viciously attacking bathers and divers, even to the extent of holding a man under water until he drowns, but none of these tales has ever been substantiated. Divers are frequently searching for the same sort of food as morays – crustaceans and molluscs – and a man probing about a coral reef may inadvertently disturb a moray, lurking unobtrusively in its lair, or may find himself in direct competition for the same prey. A man's hand may even be mistaken for suitable moray food – a small octopus for example. Under these circumstances, or when a moray is molested or attacked, some sort of encounter is almost inevitable, and some divers have sustained severe wounds.

Morays are carnivorous, and will eat anything, dead or alive, that they can find. They bolt their food whole, because they need to keep a continuous flow of water over their gills.

▶ Triggerfish

Triggerfish are natives of tropical waters, for only in the warm seas are such bright or even gaudy colours and patterns found. Triggerfish are found in coastal waters of tropical and sub-tropical seas around the world. Three species are shown here: at the top, the Pacific triggerfish, the spotted triggerfish, in the middle, and the queen triggerfish, an inhabitant of the Atlantic and Indian oceans.

The body of the triggerfish is covered with small bony plates, each of which bears one or more small spines. The pectoral fins are reduced in size, and the pelvic fins are little more than short, sharp spines. Of the two dorsal fins, the first is spinous and more or less rigid, although it can be raised or lowered. Thus, with these modifications to the body and some of the fins, the triggerfish must depend on its second dorsal, tail and anal fins for propulsion through the water. Therefore, as might be expected, it is not a strong swimmer and does not manoeuvre easily. The first dorsal fin has an interesting adaptation. There are two or more strong spines, and the first of these cannot be depressed when erect unless the second is also lowered. This is accomplished by a simple but ingenious interlocking device. Thus, when threatened, the triggerfish can take refuge in the rocks or corals, and with its dorsal and pelvic spines, make it impossible for a predator to pull it out.

Squirrelfish

There are about 70 species of squirrelfish, natives of tropical seas and most frequently found in shallow water. These two photographs are of a small shoal of Myripristis (below), found in the Red Sea, and of a single Hawaiian striped squirrelfish, Holocentrus zantherythrus. They get their name from a rather tenuous resemblance to squirrels, in that they are usually red and have large eyes. Squirrelfish are nocturnal. During the daylight hours they conceal themselves in cracks or openings in coral or other appropriate hiding places. They are highly territorial animals, defending their area against intruders and sending loud warning calls to advertise their presence and attract mates. The call is produced by the vibration of muscles which are attached to the swim bladder, which acts as a resonator to amplify the sound, frequently loud enough to be heard above the water.

Because of their nocturnal habits they have good eyesight and protective spines, seen particularly well in the photograph of the striped squirrelfish. The adults have few enemies, except for commercial fisheries in some areas, particularly in the Pacific. They are highly predatory fish, and this is probably one of the reasons for their pronounced territorial behaviour, so that they are spread out over the area they inhabit and do not compete for food.

Their only vulnerable stage is when they are young. The newly-hatched larvae swim to the surface and become part of the planktonic fauna. At first they have no spines, and are at the mercy of the currents. Many larvae and young squirrelfish are eaten by predators, particularly tuna. The squirrelfish are thought to be among the more primitive teleost fish, because they have retained several anatomical features of their ancestors. Because they conceal themselves during the day and because of their protective spines and nocturnal habits, the adults have few enemies.

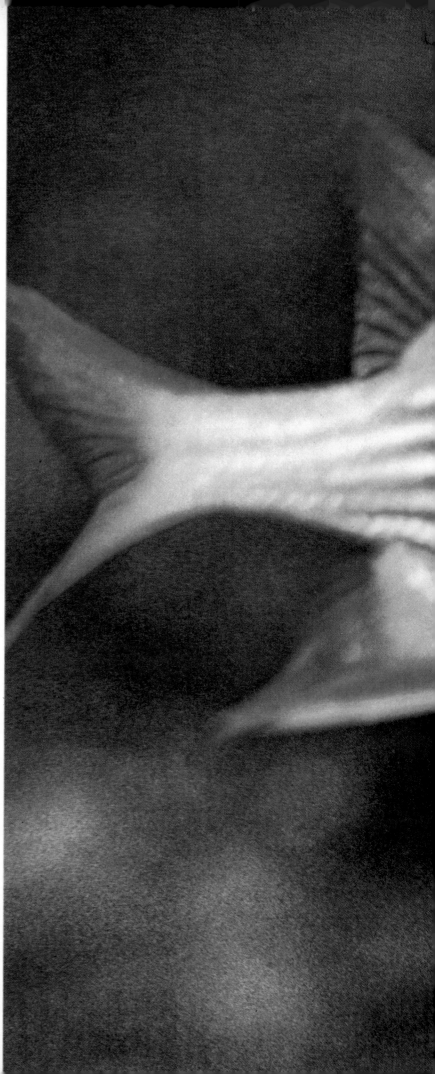

Lilo Hess

◄ Archerfish

The derivation of the name archerfish is described better in this superb photograph than any written description could possibly attempt. The jet of water droplets is achieved by a rapid closing of the gill covers, forcing the water in the mouth along a groove in the roof and ejecting it through a narrow opening of the mouth. The method by which the archerfish takes aim and hits its target accurately is quite complex. The accuracy of the archerfish's markmanship has been shown to increase with practice and with age.

There are five species of archerfish, found in the oceans of south Asia, from India through to Australia. They are members of the perch family. They are not entirely marine animals, as they inhabit both brackish and fresh water, but as the adults return to the sea to breed, it is possible they were once confined to salt water.

▼ Toadfish

The toadfish is so-called because of the shape of its head and the loud foghorn-like noise that it makes. There are more than 30 species of toadfish, most of which are found in shallow tropical and temperate seas, although some are found in brackish waters and a few are found in fresh water. They spend most of their time lying on the bottom, and may move so infrequently that they become covered with silt and debris which settles on the bottom. They are territorial animals, vigorously defending their own small areas against other toadfish or any other animal which ventures near them. The loud grunting noise they make is probably part of this territorial behaviour, as well as functioning in the breeding season to attract a mate. Eggs are laid in a sort of nest in any covered or protected areas, and are aerated and protected by the male toadfish until they hatch.

▶ Trunkfish

The trunkfish is one of the strangest of all the bony fish. Some people have described it as rather turtle-like, not only because of its appearance, but also because of its structure. Trunkfish, also known as boxfish or cofferfish, have their bodies enclosed in a protective covering of closely adjoining six-sided bony plates, leaving only the fins and the tail unprotected. The body has become foreshortened, the head blending into the trunk, the mouth reduced to a small round hole, armed with powerful crushing teeth. The pelvic fins have disappeared, and the number of vertebrae in the backbone considerably reduced. The long anterior and posterior spines provide additional protection as do the horny ridges along the back of the animal. The gill slits, the openings of the gill chambers to the exterior, have decreased in size, thus reducing vulnerability. The box enclosing the animal is so rigid that only the tail, fins and lips are capable of independent movement. Trunkfish are found at, or near, the bottom of warm marine waters, especially in the tropics, in all parts of the world.

It is obvious from this photograph that the trunkfish is anything but streamlined. The large blunt head produces considerable resistance as the fish moves through the water. Combined with this is the inflexibility of the body. Most fish use side to side movements of the body, by the flexion of the powerful body muscles, to provide much of the thrust for forward movement, but because the trunkfish lacks this flexibility, it has to rely mostly on the movement of its tail to propel it. This results in rapid and seemingly laboured tail movements, so that the trunkfish has to make considerable effort to cover a relatively short distance at a very slow rate.

Fortunately for the trunkfish, however, rapid movement is not necessary when it is so heavily armour plated. It has other protective mechanisms as well. One of these is the ability to undergo rapid and dramatic colour changes. One species found off the coast of America is green with blue spots and lines, but it can change this to a yellow background with blue spots or brown with light blue, or even at certain times, become almost completely white. In other species, there is considerable sexual dimorphism, that is, the males and females of the same species may have different colours or markings, in the same way as many species of song birds. The young fish of these species may also be differently coloured again, attaining the adult coloration with sexual maturity.

This bright, often gaudy colouring is probably a warning to other fish to steer clear of trunkfish. Not only are they almost invulnerable, but studies in laboratories indicate that some species of trunkfish release into the water a kind of poison, toxic to other fish. The source and nature of this poison is not known, but other fish sharing an aquarium with a trunkfish soon become distressed, come to the surface to gulp air, and die soon afterwards. The poison is a persistent one, remaining in the tank after the trunkfish has been removed. Other trunkfish are not affected by this poison and some robust fish, such as the moray eel, are also immune.

They eat small crustaceans, molluscs, worms and other small invertebrates, which some species catch by blowing jets of water into the sand on the seabed. They also eat the polyps of corals which are very common in the tropical waters they inhabit.

Scat *Scatophagus argus*
*The number of species of scat is not known exactly.
There are certainly three, and probably not more than
six, but it is difficult to tell, because all the features used
to distinguish them are so variable. The background
colour of the scat varies through greenish, bluish to
brownish shades of silver, and spots may be scattered, in
rows, or run together in lines or incomplete bars. The
colour of the spots or lines is also variable. There is some
evidence to suggest that these colour changes are related
to age. Scats are found in the oceans south of Asia, from
the east coast of India to New Zealand, in relatively
shallow coastal waters. One isolated species, the African
scat, is found along the coasts of East Africa and
Malagasy.*

Scat

Scat are commonly thought of as inhabitants of marine coastal waters, but in fact they spend much of their time in estuaries and in fresh water. The young especially, frequent waters of less salinity than the sea, and remain there until they are fully grown, returning to the sea to breed. Whether or not they were originally marine fish which were able to adapt physiologically to a partly fresh water existence, or whether they were fresh water inhabitants who were able to invade the sea, is hard to say, although it seems likely that the former is the more logical suggestion. Little is known of their breeding habits, for they have not been studied to any great extent in their natural environment. Although they make good aquarium fishes, they have been bred in captivity only once, and the young did not survive. Eggs are laid in rock crevices and other protected places, and it is thought that at sea they probably lay their eggs in coral reefs. Both male and female guard the eggs and young larvae, who for a short period in their lives have a heavily-plated head and neck, but this protective covering is lost as the fish matures.

They tend to browse when feeding, and appear to eat almost anything – plants, dead animals, mud, decomposing refuse and raw sewage which is dumped untreated into the sea over much of their range. Little is known about their natural enemies, but presumably larger carnivorous fish take their toll.

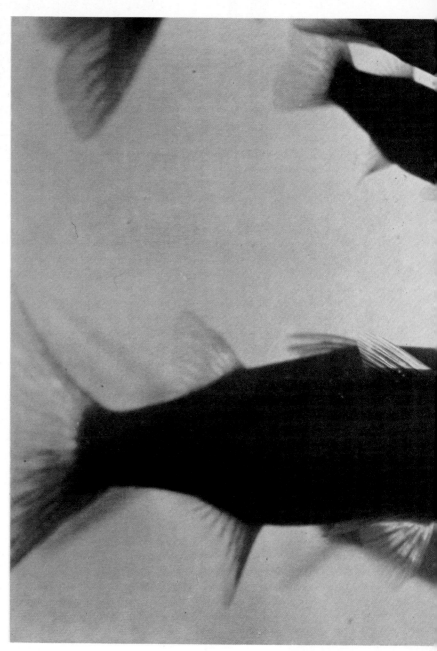

Flounder *Platichthys flesus*

The flounder (above and far right) is one of the European flatfish. It is a bottom dweller, found in shallow seas.

A newly-hatched flounder looks like any other young fish. Its body is rounded, the fins are normally distributed, and there is an eye on each side of the head. But during the next few months a remarkable series of changes takes place. The jaws become twisted, and the dorsal and anal fins, normally relatively small and concerned solely with balancing, begin to grow and finally come to extend the full length of either side of the body. The pectoral and pelvic fins become reduced in size, and the extended dorsal and anal fins become the principal swimming organs. The body becomes flattened and the flounder comes to lie on one side, with what was the right eye uppermost. Most amazing of all, the left eye migrates around, over what was the top of the skull, until it comes to lie alongside the right eye. This remarkable series of changes, which also occurs in the plaice, the dab and the turbot, adapts the flounder for its bottom dwelling habit, giving it the overall outward shape of the quite unrelated skates and rays, and a definitely lopsided physiognomy. Like many bottom dwellers, flounders are able to change colour to some degree to match the bottom on which they lie. They also are able to spend a great deal of time in fresh water, being able to cope with the problems of decreased salinity, but always return to the sea to spawn. They migrate to particular spawning grounds and do not feed on the journey.

Young flounders eat small molluscs but the adult fish have a varied diet, changing as they move from the sea to fresh water. The teeth in the lower jaw are well developed but those of the upper jaw are very feeble. However, they have crushing teeth located in the throat.

◄ **Mullet**

Mullet are able to move from salt water to fresh water via estuaries, by a physiological mechanism, not completely understood or explained, which allows them to adjust to varying degrees of salinity. This ability is sometimes used for commercial exploitation. Barriers are built across the tidal zones of rivers and lagoons which allow the young mullet to enter but not to escape. In these enclosures, they are farmed and harvested when fully grown. They are difficult to catch, for their delicate mouths tear easily when hooked. Their remarkable jumping ability, combined with the fact that when one mullet jumps all the rest in the shoal follow suit, makes even netting them difficult. Individual mullets in a shoal are sometimes seen swimming upside down.

Blenny

The blennies (left and right) are numerous fish living in shallow tropical and temperate seas. The number of species is not certain but there are at least 20 different families of blennies and each of these has a number of species. They are small fish with elongated bodies. Blennies frequently get caught by the ebb-tide, but are able to survive these periods out of water by sheltering in damp places under stones or seaweeds. Some species are even capable of withstanding long periods out of water, and have been known to climb out of the water voluntarily to sit on rocks or other structures. They are able to extract atmospheric oxygen from the air because of an enlarged thyroid gland, which in some way brings about a hormonal change which allows the blenny to exist for some time in the open air.

▼ **Porcupine Fish**

This is yet another bony fish whose resemblance to a terrestrial animal has given it its colourful and highly descriptive name. Normally, these fish have an ordinary appearance, but when they are distributed or frightened, they draw in large quantities of water, swelling their bodies and erecting their spines, presenting a formidable challenge to a predator.

73

◀ Goby

Gobies are among the smallest of the bony fish. There are more than 500 species of goby, distributed all over the world, mostly in marine waters, although a few species are found only in brackish areas and estuaries. Their most notable distinguishing characteristics are their flattened heads with large, high-perched eyes and shortened snouts, and their forward displaced pelvic fins which are joined together to form a sort of sucker.

Gobies are bottom dwellers, seeking out hiding places for homes under rocks or debris. Some dig small burrows and others hide out among the corals. A few inhabit beds of seaweed and a handful of species live in shoals in shallow open water. They feed on small invertebrates, especially crustaceans, and will also eat any carrion they find. At the time of breeding, male gobies become highly territorial, defending the area which will become the nest in which the female will lay her eggs. Fertilization is internal, and the female, guarded by the male, lays her eggs in a clump, in which each one is fastened by a short stalk to a rock or other suitable surface. The female then leaves, and the male remains to guard the nest, driving off any intruders or possible predators, until the young hatch and disperse.

▶ Cardinal Fish *Apogon nemoptera*

The name cardinal fish includes a large number of small, related species, most of whom are found on coral reefs, mostly in the Pacific. The group takes its name from the earliest discovered members, which are bright red, but many members of the group, such as this pyjama fish, have only small amounts of red or none at all.

Cardinal fish readily assume associations with a variety of sedentary animals. Conches, corals and sea urchins are favourites, presumably offering protection, shelter and in some cases food, when the cardinal fish is able to feed on the bits and pieces thrown off by its associate.

Cardinal fish are listed among a large group of fishes which have in common the behavioural characteristics of so-called mouth breeding. In such species, one parent, usually the male, will keep the fertilized eggs in its mouth until they hatch. In some species, this behaviour occurs only when danger threatens, in others they are retained all the time. Both parents may share the duties in species in which the egg-holding is done only intermittently. The number of eggs held varies with size. In one Mediterranean species, up to 22,000 eggs may be held by the male. In some species of cardinal fish, newly-hatched young may return to the parent's mouth from time to time for shelter.

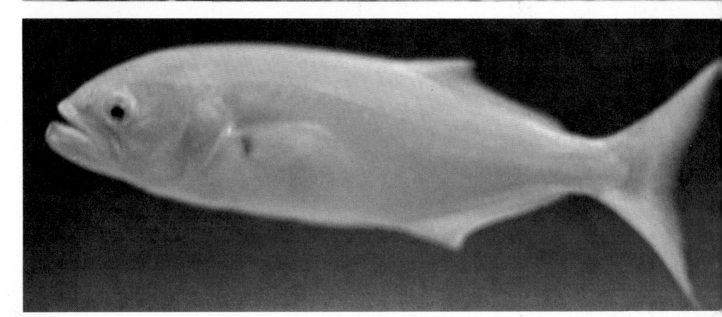

◄ Wrasse

Although brilliantly coloured, the wrasses are somewhat unique in that many of the 600 species are not tropical, but are found in colder, temperate seas, such as the coastal waters of Europe and North America. Above is an Atlantic bluehead, Thalassoma ruppelli, and below is a cuckoo wrasse, Labrus mixtus. One interesting aspect of this coloration is that it varies with sex and with the age of the individual, and can apparently vary from time to time, for example changing colour and pattern during courtship and mating. Wrasses are for the most part solitary fish rarely forming schools except for spawning aggregations in a few species. Like most solitary animals, they are highly territorial and very aggressive and will attack the fins and eyes of intruders. The male, or sometimes the pair, will build a nest of tangled weeds and other materials, or dig a shallow trough in the sand in which to lay the eggs, but, in spite of their territorial behaviour, wrasses do not appear to guard the eggs, but desert the nest as soon as the eggs are laid.

► Sole

The sole is another marine flatfish which, like the flounder, has come to lie on its left side, the mouth, fins and eyes adapting their positions and functions accordingly. The sole is best-known as a food fish and some people think that it makes the best eating of all fish. The sole is a bottom dweller of shallow seas with sandy or muddy bottoms. It prefers warm water, but some species are found either in northern or deep cold waters. The sole is a nocturnal animal. By day it lies in a trough on the bottom, which it digs by flapping its body up and down in a wave-like motion, at the same time stirring up mud and sand which settle on top of the animal and give it additional camouflage. It feeds entirely on bottom-dwelling animals – worms, crustaceans and molluscs – but is incapable of pursuing its prey and eats whatever it happens to encounter, rather than actively searching it out.

◄ Bluefish *Pomatonus saltatrix*

The bluefish is a medium-sized marine teleost, which lives in schools in tropical and sub-tropical waters. It is one of the most ferocious fish, attacking almost anything. It is therefore a popular game fish as well as an important part of many commercial fisheries. It has been extending its range in recent years, and has invaded the Mediterranean since 1945.

▲▲ Snapper *Lutjanus kasmira*

Snappers are found in warm seas in all parts of the world. There are more than 250 species. Some are important food fishes, both for commercial fishermen and sportsmen. They tend to move about in small shoals of about 12, as is this group of Indian ocean snappers, searching for food on a coral reef. They are night feeders on the whole, actively pursuing living prey, although it appears that they will eat almost anything. They are known to eat representatives of almost every class of marine invertebrate, as well as large numbers of smaller fish, underwater plants and organic wastes. The bulk of the diet seems to vary with what is most abundant, rather than having a particular type of preferred food. Little is known about the snapper's breeding habits; different species seem to have different breeding patterns. Some breed only once a year, others twice, while yet others seem to be able to breed throughout the year. In some regions, snappers have a reputation for being poisonous and therefore inedible, but this is probably due to their occasional habit of eating a particular alga which can cause cramps, nausea and even temporary paralysis, or by their eating an herbivorous fish which has fed on the alga, rather than it being a function of some poison produced by the snapper itself.

◄▼ Sole

This is a photograph of a metamorphosing sole, about sixteen times life size, in which the migration of the left eye up to the right side of the body is not yet quite complete.

► Angelfish *Pomacanthus paru*

Angelfish are relatively well-known, but as this name is commonly applied to three different groups of fish, it is important to distinguish just which group is being discussed. One, the most commonly encountered, is freshwater, and is a favourite with aquarists. Another is a relative of the sharks, and therefore an elasmobranch, and is sometimes called the mouthfish as well as the angelfish. The third is a group of marine angelfish. The marine angelfish, and their near relatives the butterfly fish, together number about 150 species. They live mainly in warm shallow seas, singly or in pairs, around reefs, rocks and corals. A few species enter estuarine waters. Angelfish are most notable for their bright colours and patterns. Colours and patterns may differ with age or between the sexes. This photograph of a French angelfish shows the kind of coloration as well as the rather bizarre form of these fish. The small mouth is armed with strong teeth, used for crushing the small invertebrates on which angelfish feed. The reason for their bright colours and complex patterns has not been fully explained. They are not aggressive, dangerous or poisonous, so it seems unlikely that this display is intended as a warning to predators. On the contrary, it is reasonable to assume that angelfish call attention to themselves in this way, and that this method of finding a mate outweighs the disadvantages of attracting predators.

◄ **Surfperch**

The surfperch is very similar in most respects to its near relatives the freshwater perches. There are about 25 species which, for the most part, live in shallow seas, although some are occasionally found in tidal pools, others at depths of up to 100 fathoms and at least one species invades fresh water. Two species inhabit the coastal waters of Japan and Korea; the rest are found on the Pacific coast of North America, from California to Alaska. The breeding habits of the surfperch are quite extraordinary. The young males are sexually mature at birth, and mate with the immature females when only 2 days old. The sperms are retained by the female until she reaches maturity soon after. The sperms then fertilize the eggs while the latter are still in the ovary, and the fertilized eggs are released from the walls of the ovary and are retained within its cavity while they develop. Embryonic development is rapid. A gill opening soon develops, and cilia surrounding and lining it drive a current of liquid into the primitive digestive tube. In this way the embryo derives its nourishment and its oxygen. Later as the fins develop, they too absorb food from the ovarian fluid, and finally the young surfperch, now able to feed, eat some of the cells lining the ovarian cavity, as well as any remaining sperm. Thus the surfperch is unique among marine teleosts, in that it has internal fertilization, embryonic development in the ovarian cavity, gives birth to live young, of which the males are already sexually mature, and it practices delayed fertilization.

 ► **Hatchet Fish**

There are two types of hatchet fish, marine and fresh water. There are 15 species of marine hatchet fish, which are distant relatives of the salmon. They are all small and weigh only a few grams on average. This photograph does not show the reason for the name hatchet fish. The head is large, and is merged with the larger body; the tail is narrow, and seems not to belong to the fish. The overall impression in a sideways view is that of a hatchet. As might be assumed from their prominent eyes, hatchet fish live in the twilight zones of the ocean, from 50 to 260 fathoms in all warm and temperate seas. Their eyes are at least as sensitive as the human eye, and are probably extra-sensitive to the blue and green rays which penetrate to the depths at which they live. It has been suggested that the hatchet fish's eyes may even be telescopic, but there is no direct evidence for this. Like many animals living at great depths, the hatchet fish has light-producing organs. These are on its abdominal region, but the reason for their presence is not clear as the eyes are so high-set on the head that it is doubtful that they could see any light produced by that part of the body.

Birds and mammals

With retrospective knowledge about the evolution of the vertebrates and their colonization of the sea on two separate occasions, first by the elasmobranchs and then by the bony fish, it seems inevitable that the next step would be the conquest of the land. This was inevitable but it was a long, slow process which took millions of years. The transition from fresh water to land was a momentous step, opening up whole new areas for the vertebrates to exploit. It was also very difficult because conditions in the air are so different from those in the water. Air does not provide water and salts and its abundant oxygen must be extracted from it in a new way, and so major physiological and anatomical changes became necessary. Air does not have the constant temperature of water, so that an animal living on the land has to be able to cope with large changes in the ambient temperatures.

There is not the space to discuss fully the slow conquest of the land by the vertebrates. A small specialized group of bony fish gave rise to the amphibians, the first vertebrates to exploit the land. The reptiles which arose from them were the first group of vertebrates to free themselves entirely from the water. The amphibians were tied to the water for breeding, but the reptiles, with the development of an egg which was covered by a tough protective shell, were not. The reptiles however, had one major problem. They could not exert any particular control over their body temperatures, so that they and the amphibians were restricted to areas which were warm enough to support life. The birds and mammals, both of which arose from reptilian ancestors, solved this problem. They are able to maintain a high body temperature which is independent of the environmental temperature, and this has made it possible for them to exploit almost every known ecological niche.

This exploitation of all parts of the environment is known as adaptive radiation, and in the course of this process it was only a matter of time before some birds and mammals acquired specializations which allowed them to return to their ancestral aquatic home. The most aquatic birds, the penguins, have become flightless in the process of becoming aquatic. The vast range of mammals – seals, walruses, sea lions, whales and so on – will also be discussed. Their adaptations to aquatic life have been many. They have become fish-like in many ways, an example of convergent evolution. For the most part, the truly marine birds and mammals are confined to polar regions, where competition from other animals is minimal or absent.

Weddell Seal *Leptonychotes weddelli*
There are four species of Antarctic seal, of which the Weddell seal is the best known. Part of the reason for this obvious from this photograph. They are not afraid of man and are easy to approach. Also, they breed near the coastline and live under the relatively transparent sea ice, so they have been quite easy to study.

▶ **Sea Lion** *Eumetopias jubatus*
There are five species of sea lion, most of which are found in the region of the Pacific Ocean. Their breeding grounds are along the western coast of North America, the northern coasts of Alaska, Japan, China and Russia, the southern coast of Australia, the Galapagos Islands and the west and east coasts of South America. This is a photograph of a rookery of the Steller's sea lion, along the North American coast.

▼ **King Penguin**
The king penguin is another Antarctic species, and is often confused with the emperor penguin, a near relative. The king penguin is the smaller of the two, and is distinguished from the emperor penguin by the size and shape of the yellow patches on the side of the head. The king penguins have a wider range than the emperors, living as far north as the ice-free seas around the Falkland Islands. They live at sea when not breeding, and can swim long distances.

◄▲ Pilot Whale

The pilot whale is a large dolphin which may reach a length of up to 10m. There are several species of pilot whales, which are black except for a white patch under the chin. They live in large schools which may number hundreds or even thousands of individuals. The name comes from their follow-the-leader habit, and it has been suggested that a single dominant male may lead each pack, but it seems more likely that the pack will follow whichever animal is in front at any time. Pilot whales are armed with strong teeth which they use for securing their prey. They eat mainly squid and cuttlefish, although some bony fish probably make up a part of their diet. Schools of pilot whales migrate annually, moving north in the summer after new food sources, and south in the winter as the water becomes colder. They are found in all parts of the world, including the Mediterranean, but are absent from the cold polar seas.

◄▼ Rorqual Whale *Balaenoptera acutirostrata*

There are four species of rorquals or fin-backed whales. They are close relatives of the blue and humpback whales, and the three types are generally known as baleen or rorqual whales. This is a photograph of one of the rorquals, the mink or lesser rorqual whale. Rorquals live in schools of up to several hundred animals, although groups like this are rarely seen nowadays, since the baleen whales have been the most severely depleted by over-fishing. Although they are common in the polar regions, most rorquals migrate to warmer waters in the winter, congregating in areas where food is plentiful, returning to the colder regions in the summer, although some individuals seem to stay in warmer waters throughout the year. Rorquals feed in two ways. Those which gulp their food do so by taking a mouthful of water, shutting the mouth and expelling the water through the baleen. Other species sieve their food by rushing through the water with their mouths open, the water passing rapidly through the baleen and the food catching in it. When they have a mouthful, they shut their mouths and swallow.

► Beluga *Delphinapterus leucas*

The beluga, along with the narwhal, forms one of the sub-divisions of the dolphin and porpoise family. They are the most easily identified of all the cetaceans, because they are the only all-white members of the group. Until about four years of age, they are grey or mottled white, but soon lose this coloration. They are natives of the seas around the North Pole, although in severe winters they move south, and have been seen in Scotland, Ireland and Japan. Belugas are toothed whales, and feed on shrimps, cuttlefish, crabs and a variety of bony fish. They were once numerous, with herds of up to 10,000 animals being reported, but they too have suffered from overfishing and herds now number about 12 or so. They have few natural enemies, other than man, the principal one being the killer whale, who will attack a full-grown beluga, although it prefers to take on a smaller one if possible. Belugas are said to panic at the sight of a killer whale.

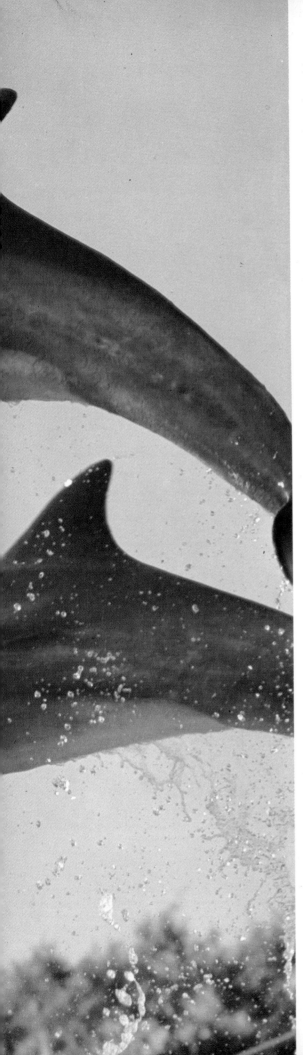

Bottlenose Dolphin *Tursiops truncatus*

The bottlenose dolphin, or common porpoise as it is known in North America, is one of the best known whales. It is the most common whale found in the North Atlantic, from the Caribbean and African coast as far north as Scandinavia. It is also common in the Mediterranean. They live in schools or packs of mixed sexes and ages, and, although there does not seem to be a leader of the pack, the males, at least, observe some sort of hierarchical organization in which some males are dominant over others. They are also noted for being co-operative animals, assisting injured members of the pack by holding them at the surface and allowing them to breathe, and providing the same sort of support for females at the moment of birth. This sociability is evident even in times of play. The jaws of the bottlenose dolphin are well armed with small teeth which help it secure and break up its food, which consists mainly of cuttlefish, bony fish and shrimps.

Like all cetaceans, dolphins are relatively slow breeders. They do not become sexually mature until five or six years of age, and the gestation period is about one year. The young calf sticks close to the mother for some time, both for feeding and protection. For the latter, the calf may also move towards an 'aunt', another female which the calf can recognize and which is the only adult that the mother will allow near her young. The young dolphin does not begin to take solid food until at least five months old, and may remain with the mother and not be fully weaned until at least 18 months of age.

Dolphins, like most other cetaceans, are powerful swimmers and jumpers. The tail is the main organ of locomotion and, unlike that of fish, moves in a vertical rather than horizontal plane. The forelimbs are used mainly for balancing. The hind limbs are of minimal use to whales.

They have a poor sense of small but very acute hearing. It was once thought that their eyesight was no use out of water, but this now seems untrue.

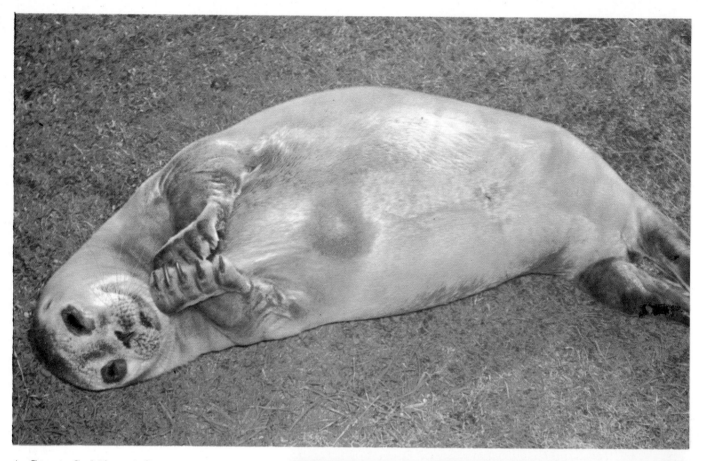

▲ Common Seal *Phoca vitulina*

The common seal is found along the coastlines of temperate and cold seas in the northern hemisphere. They prefer any shoreline where they can easily haul themselves out of the water. This is why they are particularly found in inlets and estuaries, although some herds are found on rocky, exposed costs. This photograph gives some idea of why the seal is an ungainly animal on land. The hind flippers, completely adapted to aquatic life, cannot be tucked up under the body to assist locomotion on land, so that the seal is reduced to pulling itself along with its front flippers. Seals spend the winter at sea away from the mainland, but return to sheltered areas along the coast. The pups are born quickly, at low tide, and must be able to swim immediately. They take to the water – some may even be born in the water if conditions are adverse. They spend the first few days learning to swim and dive, rarely, if ever, coming ashore.

Walrus *Odobenus rosmarus*

There are two subspecies of walrus, the Atlantic walrus and the Pacific. The Pacific ones are the larger. Walruses are found in the northern hemisphere, forming a rough ring around the Arctic Circle. Herds which live farthest north migrate south in the winter, returning to their northern grounds to breed in the summer. Walruses are social animals, as these two photographs show. Large herds, composed of families of 100 animals or more, are found, like the one on the right. The herds are made up of cows, calves and young bulls. Adult males form separate herds and come into contact with other walruses only in the breeding season. Large herds were once common, but persecution by man has reduced their numbers, and the remaining walrus herds are tending to avoid land and keep to the ice floes. Strict conservation has saved the Pacific walrus but the Atlantic subspecies is still in danger.

Adélie Penguin *Pygoscelis adeliae*

The Adélie penguin, along with the emperor penguin, is found only in the Antarctic. Some other species of penguins are also found there, but they are occasional visitors who spend most of their time and have their breeding grounds further north, some species being found as far north as the Equator. Penguins are birds of the southern hemisphere, however, and are not found in the Arctic. All penguins are flightless birds, more comical than clumsy on land. They are superbly adapted, physically and behaviourally, to their sub-zero habitat. Penguins spend much of their time at sea. They are excellent swimmers, the wings having become adapted as flippers, the body shaped hydrodynamically. Feather structure is adapted to this aquatic life and beneath the skin is a thick layer of blubber, which not only insulates the penguin, but provides a source of food during periods when the bird is not feeding. The penguin is a gregarious bird, coming ashore in October, at the beginning of the breeding season to form rookeries, large colonies of nesting penguins.

In the vast and desolate wastes of Antarctica, there is no food to be found on the land mass, so that all inhabitants of this region must do their feeding at sea. At the point where the warm waters of the north meet the cold waters of the Antarctic, there is a region of abundant plant and animal life, and it is this which provides the diet of the Adélie penguin. It is composed primarily of small molluscs and crustaceans, but most other aquatic animals will be eaten if they are available.

They are commonly seen tobogganing across the ice, lying on their fronts and propelling and steering with their flippers and their feet.

▶ Emperor Penguin *Aptenodytes forsteri*

The emperor penguin, as its name implies, is the largest of all the species of penguins. Their breeding grounds are in Antarctica, although in the summer they move north to feed, and have occasionally been found as far from home as the tip of South America. The adults begin breeding in the winter. Emperor penguins do not build nests, so that there is no territorial behaviour. Each female lays one egg which is incubated, apparently without great enthusiasm, by both parents who takes turns to carry it on their feet where it is covered by a fold of skin. Soon the female leaves and goes to sea, and the male is left to incubate the egg on his own for two months of the bitterly cold winter, the colony huddling together for warmth as the temperature drops. The females return to feed the chicks, the males then leaving to feed.

Penguins have no terrestrial enemies as there are no predatory land animals in the Antarctic, but weak young chicks fall prey to great skuas, and juveniles and weak adults to leopard seals in the water. The emperor penguin was once thought to be in danger of extinction but is now known to be flourishing.

Common Seal

Seals, like other aquatic mammals, are well-adapted to their almost entirely aquatic life. Their streamlined bodies reduce resistance for movement through the water. Even the external evidence of the ears has been lost, as these pictures show, to make the head as hydrodynamic as possible. The external ear is reduced to a slit behind the eye. The facial whiskers are extremely sensitive to vibrations. This assists the seal when it is hunting for food. Specially developed muscles in the snout allow the seal to close its nostrils when it dives, to prevent water from entering the lungs.

Like all other seals, the primary diet of the common seal is fish. Newly-weaned seals begin their diet of solid food with shrimps and other small crustaceans, and as they get older they add molluscs, crabs and fish. Most of their adult diet is made up of food found on the sea-bed – flatfish, gobies, soles, and the like, but seals also pursue and catch squid, mackerel, salmon and trout. It is this unfortunate taste for fish of high commercial value that brings seals into conflict with fishermen. Some seals turn to net robbing, inflicting a lot of damage on nets as well as on the fish in them. However, this damage does not prove the case for the wholesale slaughter of seals recommended by some.

King Penguin

Like the emperor penguin, the king penguin (bottom and right) has breeding problems, because of its size and the length of time it takes the chicks to become independent. Rather than breeding during the winter, like the emperor, the king penguin has solved this problem by breeding further north where the sea does not freeze and the adults have more freedom. The eggs are laid in the spring, after the males have indulged in a lot of display and courtship rituals which attract a suitable female. The nest is built but the male, who is left to incubate when the female returns to the sea to feed after laying, does not move about with the egg. He defends a small area for about two weeks, until the female returns and relieves the male. Thereafter the parents take turns incubating and feeding until the chick hatches about eight weeks after laying. Both parents share the feeding and protection of the young throughout the following winter. At first the young grow rapidly, being fed plenty of fish at each feeding, but as food becomes scarcer in the course of the winter, they lose weight. With the coming of spring and an increase in the food supply, there is another growth spurt, and the young moult into their adult plumage. Two months later when food is abundant, they move to the sea and quickly learn to swim and fish for themselves. At first they spend most of their time at sea, but as they get older they spend more time ashore, practising their courtship displays in preparation for their first breeding season. Like many large sea birds, king penguins are slow breeders. They do not become sexually mature until they are six months old, and because of the breeding schedule, and the long post-hatching period during which the adults look after their young, there is only one chick per pair every two years.

◀ Adélie Penguin

The breeding behaviour of the Adélie penguin, although similar in some respects to that of the emperor and king penguins, has its own distinctive aspects. The adults spend most of their time in the water, but come to land on the Antarctic continent in September or October. They have spent the winter feeding, and are in good breeding condition at this time. They make their way over land to the breeding grounds or rookeries which are usually located on rocky headlands. The penguins return regularly to the same breeding grounds, and on arrival each male searches out his old nest. Young males take over unused ones. The males occupy their nests, defending them from intruders and displaying at the same time. The females return to their old mates; new females, or ones whose mates have not returned, are attracted to other males by the vigorous display and defence routine. When the pair is formed, the female remains at the nest while the male collects pebbles from the beach for repairs and renovations. He takes the pebbles to the female, who builds a ring around herself.

Two eggs are laid. As soon as they are laid, the female, who has not fed for two or three weeks, returns to the sea while the male incubates the eggs and defends the nest. Within a couple of weeks she returns and relieves the male, who has not eaten for as many as six weeks, and has lost half his weight by this time. He goes off to feed for a week or more, returning to relieve the female. The parents in turn incubate the eggs until they hatch, and then take turns going to sea to collect food for the chicks. For the first few days the chicks stay under the guarding parent, but they grow quickly and soon come out to stand by the nest. When they are about a month old, they leave the nest and gather in a crèche, a sort of large public nursery for young penguins. They stay in the crèche for some time, while the parents continue to feed them. For feeding, the parent collects a chick and leads it away from the crèche. The chick is introduced to the outside world by leading it on little forays which adjust it for the time when it will leave the crèche and its parents, go to sea and begin to fend for itself.

▶ Walrus

This photograph of a mature male walrus shows well two of its characteristics. Body hair is almost completely absent, the hide being toughened and deeply folded. The only hairs left are the coarse vibrissae of the snout, whiskers which the walrus uses for detecting shellfish, a principal food. The large tusks are multi-purpose. They are used as offensive and defensive weapons and for digging food out of the mud. They are used for breaking up ice to make breathing holes. The walrus also uses them for locomotion, digging them into the ice to pull himself along, or using them like mountain climbers use hooks, driving them into the edge of the ice and then pulling himself out of the water.

Weddell Seal

◄◄ **Weddell Seal**

The Weddell seal is the mammal found further south than any others. Although they are usually found within sight of land they spend most of their time in the water, which is usually warmer than the air.

During the winter, most of their water range is frozen to a depth of half a fathom or more, and the seals must be able to find breathing holes. Natural holes are kept open and, if necessary, new ones are made by chewing through the ice with the teeth in a sort of sawing motion. This is of course very hard on the seal's teeth, and so tooth wear and damage is probably the principal cause of natural mortality.

Young seals are born in the spring. The females haul themselves up on to the ice, or sometimes the land, and the single pups are born a few days later. The pup has no insulation layer of blubber and is born directly on to the ice, going through a massive temperature drop at the moment of birth. The pup is not weaned for almost two months, and during this period the mother does not feed, but loses weight, while the pup puts on weight at almost the same rate. The male plays no part in the rearing of the pups.

Sea Otter *Ennydra lutris*

The sea otter, which is one of the largest otters, is found along the North American and Asian coasts of the Pacific. It is exclusively marine, and spends most of its time at sea, usually in small herds, within sight of land (above).

The posture shown by this feeding female sea otter (below) is a typical one. Crustaceans and molluscs, with the occasional fish, are the favourite foods, and the otter will dive down to 16 fathoms when hunting. Once the prey is captured, the otter returns to the surface and rolls over on its back, holding the food on its chest and eating it at leisure.

►► **Harp seal** *Pagophilus groenlandicus*

As its scientific name implies, the harp seal, sometimes called the saddleback or the Greenland seal, is found in the northern hemisphere, in the Arctic and North Atlantic Oceans. The large populations of Labrador and Newfoundland have been the most intensively studied. Early in the year adult seals move south as far as the Gulf of St Lawrence, haul out on to the pack ice, and there give birth to a single pup in late February or early March. The males join the females after the pups are born, and the juvenile, non-breeding seals arrive from the north soon after the males. The pups are born with a pure white coat which they keep for about a month before moulting into a grey coat speckled with dark grey and black markings. Both these coats have a high commercial value, and because of this, conflict has arisen between conservationists and sealers. Up to 300,000 pelts are taken each year. The numbers have been severely reduced so that recent controls now limit the numbers that can be taken and the areas in which sealing is permitted. As soon as the pups are weaned, they are abandoned by their parents and the entire population moves north again to spend the summer feeding.